Sandplay
and The Clinical Relationship

Sandplay
and The Clinical Relationship

Linda Cunningham, Ph.D.

Sempervirens Press
San Francisco, California, USA

Sandplay and the Clinical Relationship

ISBN# 978-0-9890074-0-5

Sempervirens Press, San Francisco, California, USA
www.sempervirenspress.com

Sandplay® is a registered trademark of Sandplay Therapists of America

Inquiries may be addressed to Linda Cunningham
at Linda@drlindacunningham.com

The author wishes to thank the following for permission to reprint material in this book.

Taylor and Francis for material from "Self Psychology and Projective Identification – Wither shall they meet? A Reply to Editors by Susan Sands." This article first appeared in *Psychoanalytic Dialogues,* vol. 7, issue 5, pp 651-66.

The Journal of Sandplay Therapy, for permission to use material from articles first printed there:

> The Oriental Carpet: The Interweaving of Participation Mystique and Projective Identification by Linda Cunningham. This article first appeared in the *Journal of Sandplay Therapy,* Volume 8, Number 1, 1999, pp. 69-74.

> Relational Fields in Sandplay Therapy by Linda Cunningham. This article first appeared in *Journal of Sandplay Therapy,* Volume XIII, Number 2, 2004, pp. 114-130.

> But Is It Kalffian? by Linda Cunningham. This article first appeared in the *Journal of Sandplay Therapy,* Volume XVI, Number 2, 2007, pp. 31-37.

> Countertransference in Sandplay: The Heart and the Mind of a Loving, Attuned Other. *Journal of Sandplay Therapy,* Volume XX, Number 1, 2011 pp. 105-114.

Sandplay
and the Clinical Relationship

In the countertransference experience, the image is being made flesh.
Where that means that the Other (the patient's psyche) is becoming
personal (in the analyst's body), I would conclude that an analyst's
counter-transference may be further understood by regarding it
as a religious or mystical experience.

— Andrew Samuels, 1989

For Katharine, a gentle warrior

Contents

Acknowledgements

When my adult clients enter my therapy room for the first time and see the figures on my sandplay shelves, their first comment is likely to be, "Oh, you work with children!" I explain that I only work with adults, and that what they're seeing is related to sandplay therapy, a powerful form of therapy for adults as well as children. I would like to thank my clients who have ventured into the sand. Their work in that sacred place has taught me much, and I feel privileged to have accompanied them on their deep healing journeys through the images, sensations, and emotions of preverbal trauma. I would also like to thank my colleagues, students, supervisees, sandplay trainees, and readers of my first book, *Relational Sandplay Therapy* (2005). Thank you for your comments, your encouragement, and most of all your questions, which have helped me reframe and deepen my thinking about this theory and its application.

Special thanks go to Lynne Ehlers, Ph.D., whose knowledge of symbols is sweeping and soulful. Lynne edited *Relational Sandplay Therapy* and has been of tremendous support to me in this work. We have looked at many sandplay slides together, sharing thoughts, playing with ideas, and deepening our understanding.

I would also like to acknowledge two other Cunninghams (not related) in sandplay: Lauren Cunningham, J.A., my first sandplay teacher and founding editor of the *Journal of Sandplay Therapy,* and Joyce Camaruyano Cunningham, current editor of the *Journal of Sandplay Therapy.* My love of sandplay dates to hearing Lauren present at a sandplay conference over twenty years ago. Her poetic words and magical images of sandtrays resonated in me, and I was hooked. I first met Joyce quite synchronistically as we were standing in line to take the MFT board exam. Through tireless work, Lauren and Joyce have provided a unique forum for those of us who have new ideas and would like write about sandplay. The *Journal* has been a gift to the sandplay community and to the many authors who have published there. In its pages we find evidence for this powerful method of healing, and support for the practice of sandplay therapy as it spreads throughout the world.

List of Illustrations

Figure 1: The Blue Heart. "I sensed not only her fear underlying her need to push me away with words, but also her longing to feel loved, to have a heart connection." Field One of Original Oneness/Merger. (p. 106)

Figure 2: Self State Sandtray, conveying nameless dread. A black shrunken head sits in the middle of blue tissue paper, reminiscent of Kali and the river of death. Field Two of Twoness/Rupture. (p. 115)

Figures 3 and 3a: Self State Sandtray, conveying fear of disintegration of the self. Field Two of Twoness/Rupture, mingling with Field One dissociation. (p.116)

Figure 4: Nigredo Landscape. Abstract, unbalanced, foreboding... Field Two of Twoness/Rupture. (p. 118)

Figure 5: Nigredo Landscape. Chaos and darkness; countertransference confusion. Field Two of Twoness/Rupture. (p. 118)

Figure 6: Godzilla. "Anger of monstrous proportions was being expressed and transformed." Field Two moving into Field Three of Differentiated Oneness /Transitional Space. (p. 124)

Figure 7: Protest! The "protest" felt familiar and tolerable. Moving into Field Three of Differentiated Oneness/Transitional Space. (p. 124)

Figures 8 and 8a: The Doctor Is In. "The doctor" is becoming internalized as an experience of calm, consistency, reliability and trust. The nigredo is more integrated and rubedo enters the field. Field Three of Differentiated Oneness/Transitional Space (p. 125)

Figures 9 and 9a: Self Tray. Five turtles and a lotus blossom gather at the center. (p. 126-127)

Figure 10: Diagram: The Self in Relationship (p. 131)

Preface

Sandplay and the Clinical Relationship further expands the ideas originally presented in *Relational Sandplay Therapy* (2005). As I have worked with these ideas, I have found them to be quite helpful as a guide through difficult psychic territory, both in sandplay and verbal psychotherapy.

Depth psychotherapies value the unconscious as a source of information and healing. We have known since the time of Freud and Jung that one excellent way to befriend and connect with the unconscious is through another human being. Through deep somatic, emotional, symbolic, and spiritual connection with our clients — what I call "The Self in Relationship" — unknown aspects of the Self are drawn out, sometimes made conscious, and ultimately transformed. *Sandplay and the Clinical Relationship* concerns itself with these unconscious realms, and the deeply spiritual, necessary containing function that the therapeutic relationship provides.

Within the sandplay community, sandplay therapy in its original form as created by Dora Kalff is revered. Indeed, Kalff's emphasis on presence and spirituality is the very foundation of Jungian sandplay theory and practice. The *relational* sandplay theory in this book includes Kalff's original sensibilities within its theoretical framework and seeks to expand them. Relational sandplay theory is most useful with those issues that classical sandplay theory did not specifically address, and where new information from attachment and neuroscience research has now become available.

Sandplay therapists from all over the world have graciously told me how much they appreciate these ideas. I believe this is because trauma, anxiety and severe stress, together with the inability to self soothe, are some of the most prevalent psychological problems of our time. As clients with crumbling self-foundations due to early emotional deprivation surge into our consulting rooms, we frequently encounter nonverbal or preverbal trauma, experienced in the form of confusion or deadness in the countertransference. Since these experiences do happen in sandplay therapy, and they, too, must be held within a free and protected space, *Sandplay and the Clinical Relationship* offers an expanded model for attending to the totality of our subjective experience and using our right brain-to-right brain capacities for healing. It is my hope that relational sandplay theory and the idea of four archetypal relational fields will be a useful lens through which clinicians may further help their clients transform trauma.

Linda Cunningham
Petaluma, California
November, 2012

Sandplay
and the Clinical Relationship

Introduction

Jungian sandplay therapists have traditionally focused on three aspects of clinical work: the meanings of symbols, the importance of connecting with the Self, and the qualities of empathy and presence in the therapeutic relationship. While much has been written about various symbols and their meaning in sandplay, much less has been written about the constellation of the Self or how to work within the clinical relationship. These three areas are interwoven, *yet it is through the relational container that symbols are understood and the Self is constellated.* This book explores the clinical relationship and the nuances of the relational field — where transference and countertransference are inextricably connected — as well as the therapist's subjective experience of this connectedness. *Sandplay and the Clinical Relationship* offers an intersubjective theory for sandplay that explores in detail how to work silently within the therapeutic relationship.

Still in its budding stages, sandplay therapy generally adheres to the teachings of its founder Dora Kalff. At the time Mrs. Kalff was writing, however, neither relational nor trauma theories had been fully developed in Jungian theory nor in psychoanalysis, leaving her without the frame of reference that has immensely deepened how contemporary therapists see their role. Drawing from current theory and research, we may glean many details of how to work even more effectively in sandplay therapy by expanding and deepening the free and protected space.

Recent research in neuroscience and attachment theory has confirmed that *relationship not only builds but also actually changes the brain.* Further, through right brain-to-right brain communication, we may actually receive and experience in our bodies nonverbal signals from another person. This nonverbal body-to-body resonance can have a regulating or healing effect. Neuroscience is beginning to confirm what depth psychotherapists have intuitively known for many years: that the intersubjective connection of mind, body, and soul is real, and that it is transformative of traumatic relational patterns (Siegel, 2004).

I approach my exploration of relational connection in sandplay through an inquiry into *the therapist's experience of the relationship* — usually referred to as the "countertransference," or more currently, "resonance." Although perhaps not the best possible name for the therapist's subjective experience, the word "countertransference" has been used for almost one hundred years and is deeply ingrained in our professional culture. In contemporary theory, "countertransference" has been redefined to mean *the total subjective experience of the psychotherapist in relation to his/her client,* with emphasis on its informative function rather than on its interference in the therapeutic endeavor. Its value lies in the fact that it may be a tremendously helpful healing tool.

The Inner Search

My desire to study the clinical relationship in sandplay therapy gradually evolved from my clinical experiences of verbal therapy and of my own feelings, bodily sensations, spontaneous images, memories, dreams and passing thoughts. As I explored these subtle and often unpredictable phenomena, I found that attending to them led to an unfolding between and within my client and me, in the sense that unconscious patterns began to emerge and transform. Healing began to occur in ways I had never imagined. As I began to investigate the psychoanalytic literature on countertransference, I discovered that many others had investigated the healing value of working with these ineffable experiences in verbal therapy. Over time, I became more fascinated and amazed by the power found in understanding countertransference, the *other* royal road to the unconscious (Freud, 1900).

As I inwardly searched my own subjective experience in my work with adult clients in long-term depth psychotherapies (wherein sandplay work was used whenever the client so desired), I noticed shifts in my inner experience when clients moved from words to sand. I also realized that I did not usually notice the same intensity of traumatic, negative feelings or bodily sensations nearly as often as I did in verbal therapy. I did notice softer feelings, such as sadness or a trance-like feeling of being captivated by the sand world. I often felt moved in ways for which I had no words. But several times, I felt quite shaken as my body reverberated with the trauma implicit in the images in the sand.

I also experienced being completely baffled by several sandtrays for which no symbolic interpretation seemed possible — either by me or by my colleagues. I participated in consultation groups where symbolic interpretations of particular trays were attempted but fell flat. This puzzled me because I believe that each and every sandtray holds and makes visible patterns of energy from implicit or unconscious realms, but the meaning simply eluded us at times. These uninterpretable trays were often stark and bare, fragmented and disturbing, or strikingly beautiful yet seemingly inauthentic. Through the gradual conceptualization of the four archetypal relational fields, I found I could begin to understand these kinds of "uninterpretable" trays.

I began to investigate these phenomena by taking countertransference notes during sandplay sessions. During this period, I had several countertransference experiences in verbal therapy that viscerally grabbed my body and my mind, and would not let go for days. I was forced to live in my client's suffering and thereby come to deeply understand it. Why, I asked myself, has this so seldom happened to me with sandplay? Does the sand world itself help the therapist more easily absorb and even metabolize negative or traumatic experiences — or even perform some metabolizing itself (Cunningham, 1997)? Does the sandtray in some way "remove the therapist from the open field," as Jungian analyst and sandplay pioneer Kay Bradway (1991, p. 41) suggests, making the countertransference experience less intense? Or, am I not paying close enough attention to my own experience because through the sandplay I am immersed in my patient's world? I came to believe that *all of these factors, at different times,* were playing their part. I also began to suspect that sandplay itself may sometimes actually *activate* a symbolizing field, where empathy and meaning are free-flowing. I now firmly believe that this is true. However — and this is the main point of this book — there are times when sandplay does *not* seem to activate a symbolizing field, particularly with clients suffering from primitive anxieties due to early maternal deprivation, and this is exactly the area in which relational sandplay theory serves the sandplay therapist well.

My interest in sandplay countertransference increased as it dawned on me that almost everything I had read or heard in the trainings or conferences I had attended indicated that the therapist's experience with sandplay is almost always a positive, loving one. This positive tone prevailed until several years ago. In fact, in most published sandplay cases, details of the therapist's subjective experience are not usually even mentioned. Difficult countertransference experience is almost never — until quite recently — revealed at all. However, in the sandplay consultation groups I attend, the therapist members struggle and suffer in their countertransference, particularly when they feel that they don't understand something, or the process isn't moving, or intense negative feelings come up for the therapist.

I began to wonder if the powerful tool of countertransference was lying unused in sandplay theory, thereby limiting its healing potential. I began to suspect that this limitation of the theory could even distort the countertransference experience of many sandplay therapists. Might it be bringing awareness to particular aspects of subjective experience, particularly affectively positive experience, and implicitly disregarding other, less pleasant ones?

As I began to investigate the literature on countertransference in sandplay more carefully, I realized that in this area sandplay theory has not evolved along with contemporary psychoanalytic and Jungian theories of psychotherapy. This evolution moves us from focusing solely on the client's intrapsychic situation to *focusing on the intrapsychic as it intersubjectively manifests within the analytic relationship,* registering in the self of the analyst. This book seeks to bring to sandplay therapy the benefits of the revolutionary discovery in psychoanalysis that countertransference, the therapist's own experience in the consulting room, is potentially the therapist's most powerful perceptive instrument.

So I begin this book with an investigation of the history of the use of countertransference, to ground the sandplay clinician firmly in the history of what is now accepted theory, also supported by current neuroscience and attachment research.

The Subjective Experience of Sandplay Therapists

What actually happens in the countertransference of sandplay therapists? To answer that question, I conducted an exploration (Cunningham, 2003) that required an immersion into the actual — not merely the theoretical — subjective experience of sandplay therapists. I interviewed sandplay therapists, each having at least ten years of sandplay experience, asking about their subjective experience.

I found that the subjective experience of the sandplay therapist encompasses a full range of ever-shifting emotions and body sensations, intuitions, thinking, reverie, fantasies, memories, dreams, images, and experiential states — including numinous states. There is a general positive feeling — an "umbrella countertransference"— that often seems to hold the process. Within this common experience of delight and pleasure may flow a full and varied range of both positive and negative feelings and experiences. For the participants of this study, the pleasurable ambiance of sandplay was occasionally ruptured by difficult and disturbing experiences for the therapist. Yet, there is often a sense of self doubt and self blame accompanying these difficult experiences, perhaps because written sandplay theory has not, until now, explicitly embraced, explained, or found a way to make *therapeutic* use of them.

The Countertransference Literature

This confirmation that the subjective experience of the Jungian sandplay therapist includes a full range of countertransference experience — just like the psychoanalytically-oriented therapist — invites us to look toward the psychoanalytic and Jungian literature for guidance in our therapeutic use of self in sandplay therapy. Countertransference experience has proven to be completely unique to each therapeutic relationship — sometimes disturbing and arduous, sometimes mysterious and elusive, yet often profound and even mystical for the therapist.

In psychoanalytic and Jungian worlds, the concept of countertransference has evolved from its early construction as *interference* to its current realization as deep and important unconscious communications "from" the patient that are felt or sensed by the therapist. Depending on one's theoretical orientation, these actually may be understood as coming from the patient, from the relational field, or from the Self. Thus, the therapist needs to be exquisitely attuned to these communications, for the therapist's emotional response to her patient is a vast source of information about the patient's unconscious leading to a fuller understanding of what needs to be healed. This literature provides guidelines as to how to be attuned to one's own countertransference experience and how to find useful meaning in it.

A Symbolic/Clinical Approach

There has been an historical division among Jungian schools as to whether "symbolic" or "clinical" (transference/countertransference) work is more useful, or, indeed, more "Jungian" (Samuels, 1985; O'Connell, 1986). My investigation lies at the heart of that disagreement: countertransference is a "clinical" or relational phenomenon; sandplay is considered to be "symbolic." This polarity is a core issue within the Jungian community and an important theoretical issue in sandplay. However, many Jungians view this splitting of symbolic and clinical as a false dichotomy and prefer to think of the work as an interweaving of the two as "symbolic/ clinical."[1] When we come to think of them as a unity, there is a rich cross-fertilization of experience that does not exist when they are theoretically placed in opposing camps.

In this book I will attempt to strengthen the symbolic/clinical integration. As I present the idea of relational fields with distinct symbolic qualities, I believe it will reveal that the nature of countertransference in sandplay (where symbolic material is visible) is actually, at times, qualitatively different from countertransference in a solely verbal therapy. This difference lies in the therapist's pleasurable anticipation of "playing" in transitional space.

So I will attempt to bring together the opposites of symbolic and clinical work and of negative and positive countertransference in Jungian

---

[1] Cynthia O'Connell, personal communication, October 12, 2001.

sandplay theory, *and to hold them all as valuable.* As Jung taught us, the continual uniting of the opposites leads us to wholeness. It is my hope that this growing wholeness will be felt in our experience as therapists, in the healing of our patients, and in the evolving richness of our work.

Relational Sandplay Theory

Relational sandplay theory identifies four distinct, archetypally based fields of relational experiencing. These are the fields of Original Oneness/Merger, Twoness/Rupture, Differentiated Oneness/Transitional Space, and the Numinous Field. I refer to them as Fields One, Two, Three, and Four. Not elsewhere described in the sandplay literature, Fields One and Two are fundamentally important for normalizing, understanding, and therapeutically using confusing or disturbing countertransference experiences. These are pre-symbolic fields of relational trauma that require a new understanding, leading to an expansion of our holding in the free and protected space. Field Three is a place of fluid empathy and meaningful use of the symbol, and is the field in which the vast majority of published sandplay cases occur. Field Four is the field of numinous experiencing, which is associated with the transpersonal container for this work as well as the experience of a Self tray.

Because transference/countertransference is intrinsic to every human relationship, it appears in every session. It may be symbolized in the sandtray, or in the body and psyche of the therapist. It is often in the countertransference that pre-symbolic relational fields holding primitive experience are apprehended. With an understanding of these fields and what is needed in each, the therapist may metabolize or digest this experience through the use of a differentiating awareness of her own subjective experience. We will see that Jung, Winnicott, Bion, Racker, Goodheart, and Ogden teach us how to work therapeutically within the clinical relationship in all its possible forms, whether it is countertransferentially pleasant, confusing, disturbing or profound.

Relational Fields: Sandplay and Beyond

I offer this book primarily for therapists who work with sandplay and who may find it useful to gain a deeper understanding of the healing potential of countertransference. In addition, since I will be looking at what happens in the countertransference when a literal image (the sandtray and its symbolic contents) arises from the relational field, this investigation also provides valuable information for therapists working with other kinds of images, such as expressive arts therapists or therapists who work with dreams. These formulations may also add to the general knowledge of countertransference. The field theory presented in this book can be extremely useful in verbal therapy, as well.

It is my hope that this book might help sandplay therapists to be more attuned to our own experience, to understand it more deeply, and to be with our clients in a way that conveys this more relational understanding. Attuning ourselves to our own countertransference is a meditation and a deep investigation of our own experience in relation to the Other. The therapist's surrender and openness to receive whatever the other has to offer, including desperation, despair, and deadness, requires not only clinical sophistication and training but also a form of self-offering that is spiritual at its core.

Overview: The Structure of This Book

In Part I, I explore the evolution of countertransference theory from psychoanalytic and Jungian viewpoints. These theoretical weavings culminate in *field theory,* where transference and countertransference are seen as inseparable and co-created. When we *experience* from this perspective, a triad emerges, consisting of "the therapist's subjectivity, the patient's subjectivity, and the emerging and changing sense of the 'we'" (Orange, 1995, p. 24). Please keep in mind while reading this section that the theories I examine focus on verbal psychotherapy. However, our subjective experience as therapists extends to the image — be it internal or external. In sandplay therapy, we experience both the client's words and images, even if there is silence during the making and witnessing of the sandtray. In this exploration of countertransference theory, I mean to include our subjective experience of word, image and the relational field.

In Part II, I explore the traditional emphasis on positive transference/ countertransference in sandplay theory and provide evidence for a fuller conception of transference/countertransference involving positive and negative experience. I show how this wider view leads us to a relational sandplay theory involving a co-created transference/countertransference.

In Part III, I present a relational field theory for sandplay, elaborate four archetypal field qualities of relational experience, provide clinical examples of the flow of relational fields, and discuss their implications for clinical work.

Definitions

The definition of *countertransference* as I use it is imbedded in contemporary psychoanalytic psychotherapy: *the totality of the therapist's subjective experience in a reciprocal, interactive process* (Bacall, 1997). Implied in this definition is the conviction that countertransference provides *useful information* about the client and the relationship dynamics being activated.

The *subjective experience* referred to above broadly includes any experience the therapist has in relation to the client, such as feelings, thoughts, bodily sensations, images, memories, reveries, fantasies, or dreams about clients. These experiences will almost always include material that is related to — and resonates with — the therapist's own experience, including his or her unresolved issues.

By *sandplay* I mean the therapeutic modality in which the client uses a sandtray and figures to make a picture in the sand. Although I will be focusing on Jungian sandplay as created by Dora Kalff (1980), my investigation of countertransference and the clinical relationship may apply to non-Jungian "sandtray" work as well.

I speak of *positive countertransference* as an affectively good feeling in relation to the client, such as understanding, interest, rapport, love, or an experience of the numinous. Positive countertransference is not positive in the sense that it is morally good or therapeutic; it may actually be defensive or a block to healing. It is an experience imbued with positive affect. In other words, it feels good.

I speak of *negative countertransference* or *difficult counter-transference* to mean a negative feeling in relation to the client, or in relation to an attempt to understand the client. Often this manifests as a feeling of stuckness, impatience, frustration, deadness, hopelessness, a sense of being controlled in some way, or even anger on the part of the therapist. Negative countertransference likewise is not negative in the sense that it is morally or clinically bad; but as an experience imbued with negative affect, it is subjectively unpleasant or worse. It feels *bad*. However it may become a key factor in transforming nonverbal trauma.

Although I will be referring to countertransference experience as negative or positive, this is rarely done in the literature. The vicissitudes of countertransference are far too varied and nuanced for such a simple polarization. For clinical rather than theoretical or research purposes, this distinction between negative and positive countertransference would be counterproductive. Calling one's experience "negative" vs. "positive" tends to work against being able to use it productively or even to tease out its subtleties. However, it is implicit in analytic theory that the therapist will likely suffer as she experiences and endures along with her client. This suffering is subjectively experienced as having a negative affective quality. Because of sandplay theory's bias toward the positive experience, this distinction between positive and negative seems necessary for the sake of clarity and a deeper investigation of the polarization involved.

I define *projective identification* as a form of unconscious communication — and an aspect of resonance — which is often primitive but which may also be normative. It is a process whereby unbearable experience is "placed" in the other, in the unconscious hope that the other will return it in a more tolerable, usable form (Bion, 1962a, 1963/1977). It may be used in the therapeutic dyad to communicate early traumatic experiences that do not yet have words and have not yet been given symbolic meaning. Projective identification is a bridging phenomenon between the intrapsychic and interpersonal realms. It is sometimes understood as an emotional process needing a "hook" in the other; what already exists in the therapist is called forth. I like Sands's (1997b) softening of it as "experiencing through the other," a sometimes necessary form of communication. In a more Jungian sense, I have come to think of projective identification as the clinical version, in ordinary space and time, of transcendent functioning — a world of activated, liminal, numinous transitional space. [2]

Next, I present an overview of the history of counter-transference so that the sandplay therapist may be well grounded in clinical theory.

---

[2] This idea was introduced to me by Jungian analyst Cynthia O'Connell, Ph.D. Personal communication, February 7, 2003.

Part I

Countertransference: From Obstacle to Royal Road

Perhaps that is why countertransference is so important in psychotherapy... it can carry the other like a magic carpet and guide him to his goal.

— *Marie Louise von Franz, 1980*

In Part I, I explore the growing body of knowledge regarding the therapeutic usefulness of the therapist's subjective countertransference experience in psychoanalytic and Jungian theories, as well as new developments in neuroscience and attachment theory. I also discuss the evolution of the idea of the transference/countertransference as a relational field, and augment this idea with the findings of current neuroscience and attachment research.

Chapter 1

Countertransference in Psychoanalytic Theory

Countertransference, like the weather, continually changes,
but one is never without it.

— Stephen Mitchell, 1997

In the last twenty years, there has been an explosion of interest in countertransference, "the therapeutic investigation of places where words cannot yet go" (Hunter, 1998). Countertransference, or one's subjective experience of another person, exists in every human relationship. It is now viewed as "a normal, natural interpersonal event, rather than as an idiosyncratic pathological phenomenon" (Epstein & Feiner, 1993, p. 19). However, even in psychotherapy, this is not always acknowledged nor is it always seen as a useful idea. There have historically been theories of psychotherapy that intentionally attempt to remove the therapist from the field of subjectivity, so that he or she can remain more "neutral" and "objective." The current thinking in psychoanalytic theory regards this as both impossible and undesirable. The thrust of contemporary depth psychotherapy — both Jungian and psychoanalytic — is to see the fallacy of the therapist's being "objective" or "neutral" (Orange, Atwood, & Stolorow, 1997; Aron, 1996), and to make use of the therapist's subjectivity.

In an article on self psychology and countertransference, Northern California intersubjectivist and self psychologist Susan Sands (1997a) gives a vivid clinical example of her therapeutic use of her own subjective experience that is typical in contemporary psychoanalytic literature:

> Almost from the beginning of the three-year-long therapy, I had had the persistent feeling that I was never "doing enough" for this particular patient. It was not clear to me why this should be so, for the patient was very bright, verbal, responsive to and interested in me, and able to use the therapy well. But as I focused in more and more on my experience of him, I became aware of a "pull," like something tugging on the center of my chest. As this bodily experience became more conscious, I realized that I had in fact felt this pull from the first moment I met him. I also became more aware of a subtle counter-movement in myself to resist this pull, to dig in my heels. One day the patient started (as he often did) with, "I'm not sure what I want to do today," and we both sat there for a while in silence, staring at each other, my feeling the pull more and more. I felt myself becoming irritated and resistant. I told him, "I am feeling a strong pull to do something, and yet I'm not sure what there is to do." He responded immediately that he felt resentful about having to have all the responsibility for this relationship. He felt I was withholding, and he wanted to "demand — no command" — me to do what he wanted. Then he said, his eyes filling with tears, "When's it going to be my turn?" At this point we both felt a major shift in the therapy, that we had uncovered something that had been going on forever but had never before been made conscious. Suddenly it was easy for both of us to make the connections to his childhood, where his depressed and self-doubting mother had relied on him not only to guide himself but also to guide her and reassure her that she was being a good mother. He had felt this impossible pull all his life — as well as his resistance to it. The most striking evidence to me that we had reached a

new, more fundamental level of understanding was that, after this series of interchanges, for the first time since the beginning of therapy, my own sense of "pull" completely disappeared. (pp. 652-653)

Sands (1997a) goes on to explain:

In some mysterious way that we cannot begin to comprehend scientifically, the patient and I succeeded in co-creating in me a state in which I could "get" something viscerally about the pathogenic interactions of his childhood that he unconsciously needed me to understand. Together we unconsciously created a physical experience of "pull" in me so that I could better grasp his lifelong experience of feeling "pulled." (pp. 653-654)

Not unlike a mindfulness practitioner, Sands (1997a) demonstrates an awareness of her own experience typical for many analytically oriented psychotherapists today.[3] In fact, many writers on the subject of contemporary analytic theory tell us that any of the therapist's responses may be important for understanding the client's unconscious experience, and that all of them must be subject to the therapist's conscious attention and review. It is now widely accepted that the analyst is likely to learn much from the patient's resonance with her own vulnerabilities (Scharff, 1992). But the idea of counter-transference has gone through many transmutations on its way to its present state.

Over the past 50 years, the definition of "countertransference" has radically changed. Early analysts sought to keep all evidence of reactions to their clients out of their clinical work (Wolstein, 1988). Freud (1910) strongly recommended that analysts remove all traces of countertransference through a continual process of self analysis because countertransference would threaten the effectiveness of the analysis (Wolstein, 1988). Yet, two years later, Freud (1912) writes that the analyst "must turn his own

---

[3] It may be that in tracking the unconscious communications of intolerable affects, done so brilliantly in a relational context by contemporary psychoanalysts, the West has discovered an awareness practice that can rival Buddhist mindfulness practices. These are practices that recognize increasingly subtle contents in the "individual's" mind/body/psyche (Brendan Collins, Ph.D., personal communication, February 3, 2003).

unconscious like a receptive organ towards the transmitting unconscious of the patient" (p. 115). One year later Freud (1913) writes: "Everyone possesses in his own unconscious an instrument with which he can interpret the utterances of the unconscious in other people" (p. 320).

The roots of contemporary countertransference theory lie in Freud's (1912) statement about the analyst turning his own unconscious toward the patient "like a receptive organ." Epstein and Feiner (1993) point out that, from 1912 until 1950, there was little interest in exploring the complex processes involved in Freud's idea of "the receptive organ" of the therapist. They suggest that this lack of interest in the investigation of the therapist's countertransference is due to a rejection of any awareness of the therapist's own primitive anxiety and guilt. They further point out that in Freud's (1910, 1912) two comments —1) the necessity for constant vigilance of the countertransference because it is an interference, and 2) the importance of analyst's use of his unconscious to understand the unconscious of the patient — the two continuing and intertwined themes of countertransference were born.

To Freud, the proper analytic relationship is one between a sick patient and a healthy analyst. Therefore, countertransference indicates a need for more analysis on the part of the therapist because it was considered a manifestation of the therapist's own pathology. And, in a way, of course, it is. Our contemporary and more nuanced view is that therapist and patient are combinations of health and disturbances. Holding this truth, we can see that the therapist's vulnerabilities are the place where the client's vulnerabilities are most exquisitely apprehended. But having a countertransference experience was, for a long time, evidence that the therapist is in some way deficient — especially if the countertransference feelings were in any way negative. Even today, remnants of this attitude exist. Feelings of shame may preclude therapists from investigating or reporting their own subjective experiences with clients (Dalenberg, 2000). The earlier Freudian view is that within a countertransference experience, the analyst's objectivity is in some way compromised. Contemporary theorists agree that not only is the analyst's objectivity always and already compromised, but that the possibility of true objectivity or neutrality on the part of the analyst never exists at all. Today's psychoanalytic thought has come to see therapists' inherent responsiveness to their clients as a boon, not a detriment, to therapy's effectiveness.

In the late 1940s, clinicians began to question the notion of countertransference as "interference" and to consider the possibility that it might be a tool that would enable them to understand preverbal affect states communicated unconsciously by the client. In the next ten years, some followers of Melanie Klein[4] truly redefine countertransference as a useful device in psychotherapy, rather than a hindrance. These included London pediatrician turned psychoanalyst D. W. Winnicott (1947/1982a), and British psychoanalysts Paula Heimann (1950), Margaret Little (1957) and Wilfred Bion (1959a; 1959b; 1962a; 1962b; 1963/1977; 1967/1988). In Argentina, Heinrick Racker (1953; 1957/1972; 1968) came to the same conclusion.

Melanie Klein's (1946) introduction of the concept of projective identification deeply resonated with the psychoanalytic community. Although Klein understood projective identification as a defensive, intrapsychic phantasy on the part of the infant, over the years this idea has been extended by others,[5] especially Bion (1962a, 1963/1977). It is now a concept that explains the power of unconscious interaction between therapist and patient, bridging intrapsychic and interpersonal realms. In this phenomenon, the therapist's actual emotional experience is the result of an unconscious communication by a patient unable to tolerate certain feeling states and needing to communicate this to a receptive other. Projective identification is now understood as the most primary means of communication between infant and mother and, by extension, between patient and therapist.[6]

In 1947, Winnicott, in a paper called "Hate in the Countertransference," emphasizes that "however much he loves his patients, he [the analyst] cannot

---

[4] Klein herself was not a proponent of countertransference. The followers who overtly became so were denounced by Klein. She essentially remained tied to a one-person psychology. (Personal communication, Patricia Marra, January 15, 2013.)

[5] Projective identification is a concept bursting with ambiguity. According to Sands (1997a): "Projective identification has now received multiple definitions in the Kleinian literature and is best viewed as a somewhat general term for a number of related processes and fantasies" (p. 657).

[6] Implicit in this idea is the importance of projective identification in building attachment (Fonagy, 2001).

avoid hating them and fearing them" (1947/1982a, p. 195). Winnicott's idea of hate experienced in relation to patients helps to validate our full range of our very human emotional experience in relation to our patients. It also demonstrates Winnicott's thinking that separateness (involving hate at times) is essential in a relationship supporting development. Hate denotes that the mother/therapist has a full range of feeling for the other, not a collapse into sentimentality, allowing the relationship to creatively fluctuate between merger and independence.

Heimann was a follower of Klein until she wrote an influential paper in 1950 that emphasizes the therapist's emotional response as a key to the unconscious of the patient. She redefines countertransference as "all of the feelings which the analyst experiences towards his patient" (Heimann, p. 81). Heimann recommends that the analyst be in an open and receptive state in order to receive unconscious communication from the patient and then "sustain the feelings which are stirred in him" (p. 82). She adheres that countertransference frequently "brought the analyst nearer to the heart of the matter than his reasoning," and that if the analyst did not use what he was experiencing, his understanding would be compromised (p. 82). She says, "... the analyst's countertransference is not only part and parcel of the analytic relationship but it is the patient's creation, it is part of the patient's personality" (pp. 83). Inherent in Heimann's stance on countertransference is Freud's (1912) long unheeded advice to the therapist to turn his or her unconscious toward the unconscious of the patient like a receptive organ. Interestingly, Heimann further states that Freud made his fundamental discoveries using his countertransference as an instrument of research. As a result of this paper, analyzing via the countertransference became commonplace (Bacall, 1997). It also marked a major theoretical and personal disagreement between Heimann and Klein over the primacy and usefulness of countertransference (Grosskurth, 1986).

Klein (1952), focusing on transference rather than countertransference, in her paper "The Origins of Transference," addresses transference as "total situations" transferred from the past into the present with the analyst. These total situations include emotions, defenses and object relations, and redefine transference from direct references to the analyst to the total situations transferred from the past into the therapy room.

Little (1957) expands Klein's idea of total situations by introducing a new definition of countertransference as *the analyst's total response to the patient*. Little's definition of countertransference anticipates the currently accepted view. According to Bacall (1997), clinicians moved into a more "totalist view" of countertransference, an "all inclusive term applied to the continuum of therapist responses from the neurotically based to the unique objective response induced by that patient, all of them regarded as helpful in understanding the patient" (p. 671). Betty Joseph (1985) elaborates upon this concept of total situations thirty years after Little's paper, defining transference (or, currently, transference/ countertransference) as *a living relationship that is constantly changing*. She suggests that close attention to these moment-to-moment shifts in the ambiance facilitate psychic change more than any other factor, including interpretation.

More in-depth exploration of countertransference quickly followed the groundbreaking work of Klein, Winnicott, Heimann, and Little. Credit must go to Bion (1952/1959a, 1962b, 1963/1977) for taking Klein's (1946) concept of projective identification — which was not originally an idea about communication nor a two-person psychology — and emphasizing its function as normal, preverbal, fundamentally human primitive communication. Bion's (1962a, 1963/1977) concept of the mother as container for the infant's projected anxieties is seminal in psychoanalytic thinking. For Bion (1962a), *containment* is provided in the therapist's countertransference *reverie*. Mitrani (2001) explains:

> In his model, the mother — in a state of what Bion called *reverie* — first receives and takes in...those unbearable aspects of self, objects, affects and unprocessed sensory experiences of her infant that have been projected into her in phantasy. Second, she must bear the full affect of these projections upon her mind and body for as long as need be in order to be able to think about and to understand them, a process that Bion referred to as *transformation*. Next, having thus transformed her baby's experiences in her own mind, she must gradually return them to the infant in detoxified and digestible form (at such time as these may be of use to him)

as demonstrated in her attitude and the way in which she handles him. In analysis [we refer to this as] interpretation. (p. 1091)

In other words, through the process of reverie, the mother fully experiences and finds meaning in the primitive, wordless anxieties of her infant and returns them in symbolizable bits. Reverie is both conscious and unconscious, and over time, gradually leads to "the development of the capacity to make meaning." Reverie is "the attentive, receptive, introjecting and experiencing aspect of the container" (Mitrani, 2001, p. 1091). Through reverie, "the infant's raw sensory data are transformed into a psychological meaningful event" (Ogden, 1994, p. 47). Thus projective identification is a process by which "the infant's thoughts that cannot be thought and feelings that cannot be felt are elicited in the mother when the mother is able to make herself psychologically available to be used in this way" (Ogden, 1994, p. 44). In Bion's (1959b) words, "Projective identification makes it possible for him [the infant] to investigate his own feelings in a personality powerful enough to contain them" (p. 314).

Paradoxically however, reverie may feel like a lack of presence. Contemporary San Francisco analytic theorist Thomas Ogden (1994) explains that in analysis reverie represents "forms of psychological activity that at first appear to be nothing more than [the analyst's] own distractedness, narcissistic ruminations, day-dreaming, self-absorption," and bodily delusions through which he is able to understand important transference/countertransference anxieties (p. 9). The therapist who does not know about Bion's concepts of reverie and container/contained, and Ogden's elaborations of them, is likely to feel guilty when her mind wanders, and less likely to harness this powerful force.

Also prominent among theorists of countertransference is Heinrick Racker, for whom countertransference is a fundamental means of understanding the patient's internal world. In his seminal paper on countertransference, "The Meaning and Uses of Countertransference," Racker (1957/1972) discusses two ways in which a therapist may receive the unconscious communication of the patient through resonance with the client's internal world: concordant and complementary countertransference. *Concordant countertransference* is where we are attuned to the patient's self experience. Alternatively, through *complementary countertransference,* we may be induced into having an experience of some aspect of the patient's formative relationship with an important other, also called an internal object. Racker writes that our understanding of these two forms "prevents us [from] drowning in the countertransference" (1957/1972, p. 315). He adds that the repression of countertransference responses and the unrealistic goal of "objectivity" lead to a mishandling of our own subjective experience: "The neurotic (obsessive) ideal of objectivity leads to repression and blocking of subjectivity, validating our own myth of the analyst without anxiety or anger" (p. 309).

Our capacity for empathy may be found in an unconscious identification or alignment with the patient's self experience, what Racker calls *concordant countertransference.* Therefore, the analyst's ability to understand transference is related to his ability to accept his own experiences of his client's internal world in his countertransference and to identify with them based on his own past experience. To the degree that there is conflict within the analyst's personality, there will be difficulty in carrying out the concordant identification. When the analyst fails in a concordant identification, complementary identifications arise. These countertransference experiences are equivalent to the analyst's denial or rejection of aspects of his own self, which lead to a rejection of this part of the patient's self, as well. *Thus the analyst becomes identified with the patient's rejecting object.* But Racker's point may be that this apparent failure in empathy is in fact deeply empathic — it is empathic to one pole of the client's internalized object relationships and the relationship dynamic being activated. It is only through the countertransference apprehension of this communication that the patient can be truly understood.

Concordant identifications are not better than complementary identifications. They are in fact closely related, as one springs from a failure in the other. In any therapy, there will always be places where empathy is difficult. These places may lead to a complementary countertransference, a reflection of both parties' internal worlds, resonating interactively.

Not to be forgotten is what Racker (1953) calls *neurotic counter-transference,* which is based on the analyst's own issues. Racker writes,

"... countertransference may help, distort or hinder the perception of the unconscious processes" (p. 313). He notes that even though the perception may be correct, it may provoke neurotic reactions that impair the therapist's understanding.

Although Racker (1953) warns about the potential dangers of countertransference, he also encourages us to use our countertransference reactions, because even those of great intensity —including those that are pathological — may serve as tools. His model is important for sandplay, in that sandplay therapists seem to actively avoid a so-called unempathic stance such as complementary countertransference, rather than to embrace it and use it therapeutically.

The contributions of Klein, Winnicott, Heimann, Little, Racker and Bion converge in contemporary psychoanalytic theory, where countertransference is understood to be "the living response to the patient's emotional situation at a given moment" (Epstein & Feiner, 1993, p. 30). Their ideas of primitive forms of communication, the possibility of *experiencing through the other* a full range of feelings and experiences (even aggression and hate), and of transference/countertransference as a total situation that may be apprehended and metabolized through the therapist's reverie, transformed the way therapists view themselves and their work. The idea of the therapist's self resonating not only with the patient's self experience but also with his/her internal objects increases our capacity for empathy in its truest sense. The ideas of containment and reverie transform the way we work and are important for sandplay theory because in these views (as in sandplay) *interpretation is no longer considered the only available tool, nor even the best tool.*

Before delving into contemporary countertransference theory, I will explore the Jungian view. Both, as we will see, eventually arrive at the idea of the transference/countertransference *field.*

Chapter 2

Countertransference in Jungian Theory

In the deepest sense, we all dream not out of ourselves but out of what lies between us and the other.

— *C. G. Jung, 1973*

The roots of the rather contentious division between the "clinical" and the "symbolic" in Jungian thought and dialog lie in the history of psychoanalysis. When Freud and Jung split in 1912, Freud continued to reign over the realm of the personal psyche while Jung took sovereignty over the realm of the archetypal psyche — to the great limitation of both thinkers (Stevens, 1986). Jung's major work on the transference, *Psychology of the Transference* (1946/1966), uses the mysterious imagery of alchemy to illustrate the intermingling of unconscious processes between therapist and client. Jung notes the centrality of the analyst's psyche in clinical work, but actually uses the word countertransference only three times and gives no clinical examples (Sedgwick, 1994).

Jung (1946/1966) tells us that the very success or failure of a therapy depends on the work with the transference. But, unlike Freud, he stresses the importance of the transference and countertransference as a complex relationship. He emphasizes that, like alchemy, transference cannot be dealt with simply by reason or intelligence. In addition, Jung was among the first to state a number of clinical principles, including: the usefulness of the therapist's subjective experience; countertransference as a therapeutic technique; and the importance of the analyst's own analysis (Sedgwick, 1994). Jung sees that therapists who do not actively use the information available through countertransference deny themselves a powerful therapeutic tool (Machtiger, 1982).

However, Jung himself does not elaborate his ideas about countertransference but instead left that to his followers (Sedgwick, 1994). He turned his attention to amplifying symbolic/archetypal realms of meaning, and for many years his followers did the same. Thus, there is not the abundance of literature on the Jungian view of countertransference that there is for the psychoanalytic view; nevertheless, Jung anticipates many of the current developments in countertransference theory.

Jungian analyst David Sedgwick (1994), in the first Jungian book dedicated to the exploration of countertransference, examines Jung's contribution:

> Jung spoke of countertransference in many different ways. Early in his work he described it in a straightforward clinical manner. Later he emphasized the engagement of analyst and patient in an *archetypal, mutually transformative process...* Jung elucidated this complex analytic interaction via ideas and examples from chemistry, anthropology, alchemy, medicine (infection, contagion), mythological and shamanistic healing (the "wounded physician"), and eastern religion (Taoism—the "rainmaker"). In addition to these areas where the emotional involvement of the analyst is directly stated or implied, Jung's conceptions around intuition, empathy, dream interpretation on the objective level, analytic style and synchronicity all have bearing on the countertransference. (p. 10) (Italics mine)

Where Freud attempts to avoid the effects of counter-transference, Jung (1946/1966) makes it clear that countertransference is an unavoidable phenomenon. He uses the term "psychic infection" to refer to clinical situations where the analyst and patient have similar or complementary, interlocking wounds, and the analyst is caught in an unconscious identification with the patient. Jung (1946/1966) discusses the idea of the analyst as wounded healer literally taking over the patient's sufferings, leading to mutual analyst-patient transformation.

In contrast to the psychoanalytic view, Jung's definition of transference/ countertransference takes into consideration the archetypal level of experience. This is really not so different from any of the major psychoanalytic theorists. They all address archetypal experiences such as the basic drives toward attachment and its vicissitudes — the simultaneous longing for and fear of it.[7] But Jung named these innate patterns of struggle in development as *archetypal*, emphasizing that they are patterns shared by all human beings. He spoke of a universal pattern of experience that is filled in by the personal details of one's life.

Jung emphasizes that this archetypal view was not a substitute for the personal view of transference/countertransference (Stevens, 1986), but that it was important to consider the archetypal transference/ countertransference in clinical work. Especially in work with countertransference, it is important to understand that all of our selves are archetypally vulnerable in a way that all human beings are vulnerable. Examples are found in our needs for dependency and for autonomy, and our fears of abandonment and engulfment. These aspects of the fundamental human condition never get analyzed away.[8] They are often communicated through something like projective identification, or for the Jungians, they become "constellated" in the therapeutic relationship and in other relationships in life. This archetypal level of transference/ countertransference is often illustrated by Jungians through the use of alchemy, fairy tales, and myths.

As mentioned, Jung anticipates many of the ideas regarding countertransference in current psychoanalytic thought. In describing the

---

[7] Barbara Stevens Sullivan, personal communication, August 9, 2001.

[8] Barbara Stevens Sullivan, personal communication, August 9, 2001

bond that develops in the transference/countertransference field, Jung (1946/1966) says:

> This bond is often of such intensity that we could speak of a 'combination.' When two chemical substances combine, both are altered. This is precisely what happens in the transference. (p. 7)

Here, Jung anticipates the idea of the analytic third and the intersubjective field, both rather recent concepts in psychoanalysis. Both terms imply that the field or the background ambiance of the therapy, as well as the foreground "enactments" of the psychological past of both parties, are unconsciously co-created by analyst and analysand.

Jung (1946/1966) goes on to address the inevitability of a negative countertransference reaction for the therapist within this intense bond:

> It is inevitable that the doctor should be influenced to a certain extent and even that his nervous health should suffer. (p. 7)

Jung notes here in a footnote:

> Freud had already discovered the phenomenon of the 'counter-transference.' Those acquainted with his technique will be aware of its marked tendency to keep the person of the doctor as far as possible beyond the reach of this effect. (p.7)

Jung (1946/1966) then normalizes the inevitability of the "unconscious infection" (p. 12) of the therapist:

> Even the most experienced psychotherapist will discover again and again that he is caught up in a bond, a combination resting on mutual unconsciousness. (p. 14)

And:

> He quite literally 'takes over' the sufferings of his patient and shares them with him. (p. 8)

Related to this idea of taking over the sufferings of the patient are the ideas of the Wounded Healer archetype (Jung, 1951/1954c, 1955-56/1963, 1961b) and the Rainmaker story (Jung, 1955-56/1963). These are powerful metaphorical models that offer instruction in the use of the therapist's subjective experience. Sedgwick (1994), informed by the wounded healer and rainmaker models, concludes that "it is not only where the patient feels troubled but where the analyst also does that transformation takes place" (p. 107). He adds that countertransference must be *personal* before it is useful:

> Indeed it is in the very "hooks" and activated complexes in the analyst that enable the transference to "ground" and be worked through by the analyst's self [in the] entirety of his conscious/ unconscious processes. (Sedgwick, p. 117)

In Jung's (1961b) words, "The doctor is effective only when he himself is affected...only the wounded physician heals" (p. 134). Jung viewed healing as an art and stressed the analyst's personality in the art of healing. Samuels, Shorter, and Plaut (1986) elaborate:

> The institution of training analysis is an acknowledgement of the fact that, as a profession, analysis attracts 'wounded healers.' There is growing evidence that this pertains to all the therapeutic professions and may even be a qualification for such work (Ford, 1983). Jung emphasized that an analyst can only take a person as far as he has gone himself. (p. 65)

Thus, analysis for the analyst was paramount for Jung. *For the wounded healer, the goal of analysis is not freedom from difficult feelings, but the increased freedom to experience a fuller range of feelings* (Sedgwick, 1994). Sedgwick draws upon Harold Searles (1966/1979a), who reminds us that we will never be free from feelings such as envy or guilt. Searles 1973/1979b) writes, "It is clear to me that the analyst's inner freedom to experience feelings, fantasies and patient-transference-related shifts in his personal identity...is unequivocally desirable and necessary" (p. 279).

In addition to the Wounded Healer archetype, the Rainmaker story, often retold by Jung, captures many of the contemporary psychoanalytic ideas about actually working with the countertransference:

> There was a drought in a village in China. They sent for a rainmaker who was known to live in the farthest corner of the country, far away. Of course that would be so, because we never trust a

prophet who lives in our region; he has to come from far away. So he arrived, and he found the village in a miserable state. The cattle were dying, the vegetation was dying, the people were affected. The people crowded around him and were very curious what he would do. He said, 'Well, just give me a little hut and leave me alone for a few days.' So he went into his little hut and people were wondering and wondering, the first, the second day. On the third day it started pouring rain and he came out. They asked him, 'What did you do?' 'Oh,' he said, 'that is very simple. I didn't do anything.' 'But look' they said, 'now it rains. What happened?' And he explained, 'I come from an area that is in Tao, in balance. We have rain, we have sunshine. Nothing is out of order. I come into your area and find that it is chaotic. The rhythm of life is disturbed, so when I come into it I, too, am disturbed. The whole thing affects me and I am immediately out of order. So what can I do? I want a little hut to be by myself, to meditate, to set myself straight. And then, when I am able to get myself in order, everything around is set right. We are now in Tao, and since the rain was missing, now it rains.' (as cited in Chodorow, 1997, pp. 19-20)

This potent and poetic model emphasizes internal work within the self of the therapist. The full task of the therapist is to internally hold and relate not only to her own unconscious but to the patient's unconscious and to the Unconscious as well, while silently holding the imagery evoked in her while sitting with a patient (O'Connell, 1986).

Sedgwick (1994) explains that "the rainmaker ideal is achieved, not 'given' and follows a stirred-up countertransference feeling usually of impressive magnitude" (p. 116). O'Connell (1986) notes that it requires that the therapist be able to contain her own anxieties, and "to silently incubate the unknown without tension reducing..." (p. 109).[9] Often, this requires "little bits of working through" (Sedgwick, p. 116) and is not accomplished in one fell swoop. The silent containing of anxieties and

---

[9] This requires what Keats (1817/1973) referred to as "negative capability" — the ability to be "in uncertainty, mysteries and doubts, without any irritable reaching after fact and reason ... remaining content with half knowledge" (pp. 477-8). The idea of negative capability was an important one for Bion (1967/1988).

symbolizing of little bits of experience is reminiscent of Bion's (1962b) model of container/contained.

Even though Jung originally espoused intersubjective ideals, the Jungian view of countertransference, like the psychoanalytic view, has evolved from a stance where the analyst hoped to achieve objectivity. Fordham (1993) notes that in the beginnings of Jungian analysis, the therapist's own subjective states "were thought to be essentially irrelevant. Not much attention was paid to Freud's (1910) view that the analyst uses his unconscious as an organ of perception, nor to Jung's emphasis on the importance of the analyst's personal influence" (p. 207). This has slowly changed as Jung's followers have expanded his theory.

Michael Fordham (1957/1974, 1988, 1993), a loyal follower of Jung, fills in the gaps in Jung's model of countertransference theory. Greatly influenced by Klein, he developed a Jungian understanding of countertransference and projective identification based on tracking the subtleties of subjective experience between himself and his patients. Fordham concludes that the essential constituents of transference feelings are infantile. He encourages Jungians to pay attention to the intensity of these unconscious affects, and to analyze their "embodied quality" (Astor, 1995, p. 19). He approaches sessions as Bion (1967/1988) suggested, without memory or desire, actively using his countertransference. His study of the Self leads to his concepts of deintegration and reintegration. Fordham (1988) writes:

> In essence, deintegration and reintegration describe a fluctuating state of learning in which the infant opens itself to new experiences and then withdraws in order to reintegrate and consolidate those experiences. During a deintegrative activity, the infant maintains continuity with the main body of the self (or its center), while venturing into the external world to accumulate experience in motor action and sensory stimulation.... Such a concept of the self brings a new dimension to both depth psychology and developmental psychology, for it is now conceived to be a dynamic structure through whose activity the infant's emotional and ego growth takes place. (p. 64)

Fordham (1957/1974) tells us that as therapists, we need to allow ourselves to deintegrate spontaneously in the way our patients need us to — to feel the full force of these primitive experiences — and that these deintegrates are manifestations of the Self.[10] If we try to remain always "integrated" we are in effect isolating ourselves from the patient and from his experience.

Fordham (1957/1974) is one of the first Jungian writers to expand Jung's view of the transference/countertransference situation as a field. In this view, transference and countertransference are not separable; they form a co-created web of interconnectedness. Many other Jungian writers have since further developed field views of transference/countertransference (Goodheart, 1980; Hall, 1984; Schwartz-Salant, 1988, 1995; Speigelman & Mansfield, 1996).

Two important Jungian writers, Andrew Samuels (1989, 1993) and Nathan Schwartz-Salant (1988), focus on *embodying* the countertransference. Schwartz-Salant holds a view of countertransference based on a bodily felt relationship to the field and suggests that the deeper unconscious is constellated only through the countertransference. Samuels's field view focuses on the *images* of countertransference and projective identification. In a study, he identified three types of countertransference response —body/behavioral, feelings and fantasies — all of which he regards as *images*. Samuels (1989) explores the connection between body and image:

> The link between body and image is waiting to be further verbalized. *In A Midsummer Night's Dream,* Shakespeare wrote that 'imagination bodies forth the forms of things unknown' (Act 5, Scene 1). If countertransference communications are both images and bodily visions, then body and image shimmer together almost to the point of fusion. (p. 165)

For Samuels, in countertransference, "the image is being made flesh" (1989, p. 165). The patient's psyche is becoming personal in the analyst's

---

[10] This model of the Self was later elaborated by Gordon (1965) and Schwartz-Salant (1988) in terms of the projective identification processes involved in deintegration.

body. Countertransference may, therefore, be considered a form of mystical experience. Samuels explores the mutual characteristics of countertransference and mystical experience:

> First, mystical states are ineffable; that is, they cannot be fully described to one who has not experienced something similar. Second, mystical states lead to knowledge and insight, often delivered with a tremendous sense of authority. Third, mystical states are transient. Fourth, mystical states *happen* to a person; even if he or she prepared him/herself, he or she is gripped by a power that feels quite foreign. Fifth, there is a sense that everything is connected to everything else, an intimation of purpose. Sixth, the mystical experience is timeless. Finally, the familiar ego is sensed not to be the real 'I.' (p. 166)

Thus Samuels explains how even the "mundane," ordinary counter-transference experiences — such as Sands's example in the beginning of this chapter — may be experienced as mystical by the psychotherapist.

In a further Jungian development that is of central importance to this book's theory, Goodheart (1980) uses the work of Searles (1965, 1979c) and Langs (1978a, 1978b, 1979; Langs and Searles, 1980) to develop a Jungian view of field theory.[11] He elaborates three interpersonal fields that may arise in a therapy. Each of these fields is mutually created and may be shifting and fleeting or relatively permanent. Each holds its own unique countertransference experience, having a "totally different 'feel' to the therapist" (Goodheart, 1980, p. 4).

Goodheart's three fields are: The *persona-restoring field*, the *complex-discharging field*, and the *secured-symbolizing field*. The persona-restoring field, which Searles (as cited in Goodheart, 1980) called the "out of contact field," is a field of noncommunication in which meaning is destroyed (Langs, 1978b). The client uses words to fend off the therapist; no symbolic understanding is possible. Goodheart (1980) writes,

---

[11] The work of Langs (1978a, 1978b, 1979) constitutes the beginnings of intersubjectivity theory in psychoanalysis.

33

the use of communication in this field is to *avoid* contact while inviting the other into a mutual deception that there is contact. Therefore any "abreacting" or "remembering" or "exploring dreams" or "interpretations" or "active imagination" or "sandtray work" which takes place while this field is constellated merely serves in the mutual deception, the illusion of a therapeutic communication. (p. 5)[12]

Countertransference in this field arises from the projective identification of emptiness and nonmeaning (Langs, 1978b). Or, to use Jungian terminology, emptiness and nonmeaning become *constellated* in this field.

Next, Goodheart (1980) describes the *complex-discharging field,* wherein complexes are mutually activated in both therapist and client, and "language and behavior are used unconsciously by each partner as a means to discharge tension into the other" (p. 8). He says that the analyst identifies the presence of this field "mainly by anxiety, tension and pressure which he feels emerging within himself with or without obvious coercion from the patient" (p. 8). This is also a field of projective identification. It is the field most explored in the Freudian and Kleinian traditions.

Goodheart's (1980) third field, the *secured-symbolizing* field, "is familiar territory to Jungians, for it is the field in which the processes of symbolic transformation can occur" (p. 8). Before the work of Langs, upon which Goodheart bases his Jungian model, Jungians assumed that all analysis took place in this type of field. In this field, there is a "free mutual exploration of fantasy and reality" (p. 9), a collaborative exploration using symbols. "Empathy comes easily," along with a sense of closeness and of the "impersonal" in the relationship (p. 9). The countertransference experience of this field is a "quiet gentleness [felt] to be awesome in its power;" "a loving acceptance of the immediate relatedness with the patient;" a "childlike playfulness" and "liveliness or contentment or fulfillment" (Searles, as cited in Goodheart, p. 9). Goodheart quotes the

---

[12] In relational sandplay theory, I refer to this as Field One, and a deeper understanding of the anxieties involved here bring a symbolic understanding of this very normal psychic territory.

work of Deri (1978) on transitional phenomena to describe the subjective feel of the *secured-symbolizing space* (p. 11). It is

> ... transitional between dream and reality, between inside and outside, the person and the environment. It is par excellence the dimension of connectedness, or, even better, of mutual immanence. This is the space for creative symbol-formation, because it is the function of symbols to connect and unite opposites. This transitional space, a space for connectedness, accounts for an order in the world based on an inner relatedness instead of the Cartesian principle of dividedness. The construction of the concept of transitional space and its value for mental health is Winnicott's unique contribution to psychoanalysis. (p. 50)

Goodheart (1980) concludes his descriptions of these fields by saying that the awareness of the *secured-symbolizing field* by Jung, then by Winnicott, led to a flowering of contemporary psychoanalysis that has very little to do with psychoanalysis before 1960. Goodheart's description of the *secured-symbolizing field* has been used by Bradway and McCoard (1997) in their discussion of co-transference in sandplay, which I will further discuss in Part II.

Goodheart's (1980) description of the *secured-symbolizing field* is, in fact, very similar to the way in which sandplay therapists describe their subjective experience. It is a field of concordant countertransference and transitional play space. O'Connell (1986) further elaborates and expands the *secured-symbolizing field,* by identifying the numinous field that may arise from it, distinguishing this truly Jungian territory — the numinous *secured-symbolizing context-plus field* — as the field of the transcendent function. Whereas the *secured-symbolizing field* has equivalents in psychoanalysis, the *secured-symbolizing context-plus field* belongs to the Jungian world alone — and experientially is quite familiar to Jungian sandplay therapists.

Goodheart (1980) moves Jungians toward intersubjectivity with his conceptualization of three interacting, shifting fields of experience in psychotherapy. His model is still relevant in that it can help clinicians live through these distinguishable, sometimes difficult countertransference experiences by normalizing them. They all exist, ever present and shifting, and the countertransference experiences therein are all normal for each particular field. A large part of any analysis may be done in any one of these three fields, not just in the *secured-symbolizing* field. As we shall see, contrary to Goodheart's view of the *persona-restoring* and *complex-discharging* fields, work in any field is legitimate and necessary therapeutic work, and not, as is often thought, biding one's time until the transitional space of the *secured-symbolizing field* can be achieved.

Although the Jungian view of countertransference is a larger, less detailed perspective, there is a Jungian flavor to most psychoanalytic theory today in that it includes emphasis on the clinical use of the countertransference (Samuels, 1989). Within this Jungian flavor lies the notion that analysis is mutually transforming, that it is an interaction, and that the analyst's experience of the *feeling connection* within the transference/countertransference field is of central importance.[13]

As Sedgwick (1994) writes, "It is one thing to take note of counter-transference and another to really work with it" (p. 4). Barbara Sullivan, states, "What is crucially important about [the transference experience] is that it be lived as intensely as possible.... It is the full emotional experience that is the primary healing factor" (Stevens, 1986, p. 191). She goes on to explain that the Jungian approach holds that countertransference reactions are "inescapably present at every moment" and are the most important and immediate form of data we have (p. 192).

So Jung anticipated much of the current psychoanalytic understanding of countertransference, as well as the development of intersubjectivity theory. But for a deeper understanding of the inseparable nature of transference and countertransference, we must turn to the contemporary literature of psychoanalysis.

---

[13] Herein lies a distinct difference between Jungian and certain other psychoanalytic theories. (Barbara Stevens Sullivan, personal communication, August 9, 2001). In the latter, a disruption of a feeling connection would be noticed as meaningful; the countertransference absence of feeling — blankness or a state of feeling controlled — is an important communication. Also, one might not seem to have a "feeling connection" when involved in a complementary countertransference.

Chapter 3

The Transference/ Countertransference Field

When two chemical substances combine, both are altered.
This is precisely what happens in the transference.

— *C. G. Jung, 1946/1966*

Contemporary psychoanalytic countertransference theory often focuses on the concepts of projective identification and empathy. The concept of projective identification highlights the therapist's experience of the client *within the therapist;* with empathy our focus is on the fluctuating affective state of the other — the client. The two are experienced quite differently: "Whereas empathy is typically related to a therapist's skillful functioning, projective identification is commonly associated with counter-transference turmoil" (Tansey & Burke, 1989, p. 9). Perhaps this calls into question what is conscious and what is unconscious experience. Empathy is often closer to consciousness. Projective identification is at first clouded with unconsciousness and needs to be made more conscious. Projective identification has the feel of being *taken over* by the experience, whereas empathy is a "tool we apply at our volition" (Sands, 1997b, p. 696).

In projective identification, the patient is inducing an unconscious experience or affect state in the therapist for metabolization. This experience could be one that threatens danger to the patient's sense of integration and is preverbal and/or traumatic in origin. When there is no language with which to articulate an experience or feeling, projective identification may be the only way to communicate certain feelings or experiential states to another person, who may feel the communication viscerally. Sands (1997b) refers to this as "experiencing through the other" (p. 696).

Contemporary thinking about countertransference and transference focuses simultaneously on the experience of both client and therapist. Thus transference and countertransference have come to be seen as inseparable. The ideas of projective identification and empathy converge in some contemporary psychoanalytic theories with the idea of the intersubjective field. Many now claim that in this view the term "countertransference" is inadequate. Bacall (1997, p. 670) suggests that *subjectivity* is a better word than countertransference. He tells us that "contemporary perspectives on countertransference have virtually redefined it to denote the effects on the analyst of a reciprocal or interactive process" (pp. 670-71). In this new view, countertransference is an ongoing feature of the therapeutic relationship that has the potential not only to interfere, but also to inform. Countertransference partly shapes but also reveals the patient's transference (Wallin, 1999). Intersubjectivity challenges the assumption that the therapist can know, from a privileged position, the intrapsychic workings of the patient. Instead, the therapist's understanding gradually grows out of the interaction from direct inquiry into the patient's experience. Within this co-created field of complex intertwinings of transference/ countertransference, we are reminded of Jung's (1946/1966) ideas about "a chemical combination," which anticipated contemporary intersubjectivity.

Field Views of Transference/Countertransference in Contemporary Psychoanalytic Theory

Based in part on discoveries in quantum physics, psychoanalysis has moved toward a field view of transference/countertransference. Intersubjectivist Donna Orange (1995) describes the field view as "interplay" with "elements of emergent novelty and surprise" in which "your [understanding] and mine assume their particular shape in our relatedness" (p. 24). In the field, "the individual comprehends, or takes in, the relation, while the relationship includes, and partly forms, the experiencing and experienced self" (p. 5). Rather than focusing on a one- or two-person psychology, field theory illuminates the *triadic* aspect of "two subjectivities and the emerging understanding that contains and informs them" (p. 24). Field theory relies heavily on Winnicott's paradoxical idea of transitional space — a space that is neither inner nor outer world, self nor other, reality nor fantasy.

In field views, we no longer rely solely on words to convey information, but rather hold and value tacit and somatic forms of information as well as verbal expressions. Orange explores this implicit knowing, stating that "most experiencing is visceral, emotional and only partly organized" (p. 106). She points out that implicit knowing is echoed in Bollas's concepts of *somatic knowing:* "Experience that encodes itself in our whole being as memory," and *existential memory:* "Memory that is registered in one's being." Both are aspects of the *unthought known* — that which is known but has not yet been thought (Bollas, as cited in Orange, pp. 110-111).

I will briefly describe several field views that I believe are relevant to sandplay theory: Relational theory (Aron, 1996), Ogden's positions (Ogden, 1986; 1989; 1994), and Orange's "co-transference" (Orange, 1995).

Relational Theory

Relational theory, according to Lewis Aron (1996), includes object relations theory, self psychology, and Stolorow's intersubjectivity theory. It is influenced by feminist and postmodern critiques. Aron explains a paradigm shift in psychoanalysis that includes a change in emphasis from the intrapsychic to the interpersonal (which includes the intrapsychic); from drives to relationship; and from a belief in the omnipotent authority of the analyst to a mutual, reciprocal sharing between two people. This shift also entails a reconceptualization of transference. No longer is transference considered to be a distortion on the part of the patient, but rather a co-creation between analyst and patient. Aron also discusses the evolution of the concept of projective identification in psychoanalysis from a more mystical concept to an interpersonal exchange based on the pressure to feel a particular feeling placed on one person by another. He considers projective identification to have been a necessary bridging concept between the intrapsychic and the interpersonal realms. He describes both enactments and projective identification as continual processes rather than discrete events.

Ogden's Field View

Ogden[14] (1994) addresses the field from a stance informed by the work of Klein, Winnicott, and Bion. Ogden focuses on the ambiance of transference/countertransference, often experienced as background music. The therapist's interventions must address this transference/countertransference matrix itself. Ogden describes how he apprehends experience rather than affect. In this way, Ogden takes us beneath the affect to pre-emotional bodily states, where we may become aware of more primitive realms of human experience — both our clients' and our own.

Ogden (1994) tells us that human beings have a deep need to communicate and that sometimes this communication takes place through projective identification. He describes mutual projective identification as creating a complex system of interpersonal forces in which the analytic third is a vehicle for both thoughts and feelings to be actualized and experienced — though differently — by both therapist and patient.

The Analytic Third

According to Ogden (1994), the analytic third, rich with unconscious meaning, is co-created by the analyst and analysand. At the same time, the analyst and analysand are created by the analytic third, although this is a uniquely different experience for each, and is experienced through the therapist's countertransference. The analytic third penetrates and surrounds and shapes the experience of the therapeutic dyad, coming to awareness and eventually understood and digested through the therapist's reverie.

---

[14] Ogden does not consider himself part of the "relational" group or the "intersubjectivity" group, although he writes of the intersubjective phenomenon of the "analytic third" (Patricia Marra, personal communication, November 20, 2002).

Also fundamental to Ogden's (1994) field theory is his description of three modes of human experience, psychic states he calls "positions": the *autistic-contiguous position* (Ogden, 1989), the *paranoid schizoid position,* and the *depressive position* (Klein, 1935/1968). The analytic third is the outcome of the interplay of these three distinct modes of experiencing anxiety and constructing meaning (Ogden, 1994). Ogden's positions are reminiscent of Goodheart's (1980) three fields of transference/countertransference experiencing in that they reappear as a flow of ever shifting states of experience, co-existing as "multiple stages of consciousness" (Ogden, 1994, p. 198). Each position is a nonexistent ideal that is never encountered in pure form. I describe the three positions in some detail because I believe they are important concepts for sandplay theory.[15]

The Autistic-Contiguous Mode of Experience

The autistic-contiguous position is the most primitive of the three organizations of experience. It is generated within the experience of "mother as environment." It represents "a transferring of the internal environment within which one lives onto the analytic situation" (Ogden, 1994, p. 138). Ogden (1989) wrote:

> The autistic-contiguous organization is associated with a specific mode of attributing meaning to experience in which raw sensory data are ordered by means of forming pre-symbolic connections between sensory impressions that come to constitute bounded surfaces. It is on these surfaces that the experience of self has its origins. (p. 49)

Ogden (1989) quotes Freud, who said, "The ego ... is first and foremost a bodily ego... i.e., the ego is ultimately derived from bodily sensations, chiefly from those springing from the surface of the body" (as cited in Ogden, 1989, pp. 49-50). The autistic-contiguous position is a *pre-symbolic* mode of experience; the experiences being organized may become, with

---

[15] The reader will notice that I quote Ogden extensively. Ogden's writing is like poetry, and at times his meaning may be elusive. By providing examples of Ogden's writing, I hope to aid the reader in creatively distilling the essence for him or herself.

good enough containment by the primary caregiver, the ground for the creation of symbols. There is a rhythm to this mode that constitutes what Winnicott (1956/1982b) calls "going on being" (p. 303).

Early sensory experience consists of soft and hard edges, which will later come to be thought of with words such as "comfort," "soothing," "gentleness," or "armor," "invasion," "repulsion," and "separateness" (Ogden, 1989). Anxiety in this mode is related to disconnectedness or disintegration of one's sensory surface or "rhythm of safety" (Tustin, in Ogden, 1989, p. 68). Defenses in this mode are aimed toward refinding a sense of "continuity" and "the bounded sensory surface" as well as one's own unique rhythm of being "upon which the early integrity of self rests" (Ogden, 1989, p. 70).

Activities such as hair twirling, stroking of the face, constant speaking or humming can all be thought of as the use of shapes and edges for the purpose of self-soothing. In this position, the patient may use the therapist as a *second skin* (Bick, 1968) or container which may then gradually become symbolizable. In pathology, the countertransference experience may be likened to that of "a *petit mal* seizure, or a state of non-experience." Here, "the process of attributing meaning to experience" ceases to function (Ogden, 1989, p. 52).

The Paranoid-Schizoid Mode of Experience[16]

The paranoid-schizoid position, a more differentiated state of being, is a mode of generating and organizing experience similar to being in a Jungian "complex."[17] Here, splitting and projective identification reign. On the positive side, Ogden (1994) writes that "...the negating deintegrative effects of the paranoid-schizoid position continually generate the potential for new psychological possibilities" (p. 41).

---

[16] Ogden uses Klein's theory of the paranoid-schizoid position, and expands it into a mode of experience as opposed to just a developmental position in time or a pathological experience (Patricia Marra, personal communication, January 15, 2013).

[17] The complex is touchy and reactive, seeks expression, resists change and is repetitive. An activated complex is not under ego control and displays a distinct absence of empathy and self-reflection. It has a magnetic, inductive quality that pulls two people into Goodheart's complex-discharging field (Irvine, 1999).

Ogden (1986, 1994) describes experience in this mode as predominantly nonreflective. Thoughts and feelings "happen" to the person. There is no interpretive "I" and no symbolizing of experience. He says that splitting (of people, ideas, thoughts and feelings into all good and all bad), and projective identification (along with idealization, denial, and omnipotent thinking) are the predominant defenses. History is constantly being "rewritten" to keep loving and hating aspects of the self and object separate. This simplifies the internal world of the primitive psyche until more complexity can be tolerated (Ogden, 1986, p. 65). Ogden (1989) adds that in this mode "thoughts and feelings are not experienced as personal creations but as facts, things-in-themselves, that simply exist. Perception and interpretation are experienced as one and the same" (p. 21). He explains that this concrete mode of generating experience in the paranoid-schizoid mode "contributes to the sense of immediacy and intensity of experience" (Ogden, 1994, p. 35).

As for the nature of the transference in the paranoid-schizoid mode, it is as if the patient "has emotionally recreated an earlier object relationship" (p. 14). In the countertransference, this may be felt as a sense of discontinuity from session to session or even moment to moment.

The Depressive Mode of Experience[18]

The depressive position represents a more mature form of anxiety. Its hallmark is the ability to perceive, tolerate, and hold in mind the essential ambiguity of reality. Ogden (1994) describes it this way:

> (1) an experience of interpreting "I-ness" mediating between oneself and one's lived sensory experience; (2) the presence of an historically rooted sense of self that is continuous over time and over shifts in affective states; (3) relatedness to other people who are experienced as whole and separate subjects with an internal life similar to one's own; moreover one is able to feel concern for the Other, guilt, and the wish to make nonmagical

---

[18] The depressive position is Melanie Klein's original idea. As with the paranoid-schizoid position, Ogden uses her theory and expands it into a mode of experience as opposed to just a developmental achievement in time.

reparation for the real and imagined damage that one has done to others; and (4) forms of defense (e.g., repression and mature identification) that allow the individual to sustain psychological strain over time.... In sum, the depressive mode generates a quality of experience endowed with a richness of layered symbolic meanings. (pp. 35-36)

This description carries the positive tone of developmental achievement. Yet, the depressive mode of experience alone, without the other two modes arising as well, would lead to stagnation. *The easy oscillation of all positions is more psychologically mature than the depressive position alone.*

In a depressive mode, "transference represents an unconscious attempt to recapture something of one's experience with an earlier object in the present relationship. This ... form of transference is rooted in the context of the sadness of knowing that the relationship with the original object is a part of the past that one will never have again" (Ogden, 1989, pp. 14-15). The countertransference experience in this mode is symbolically meaningful, as psychic reality becomes more valued. There is a feeling of more psychological separateness as well as closeness, as feelings of guilt are integrated, and palpably becoming an inherent part of love.

Co-Transference

In yet another field view, intersubjectivists Orange, Atwood, and Stolorow (1997) contend that therapist and client are involved in the mutual creation and interplay of the transference-countertransference, sometimes referred to as "co-transference" [19] (Orange, 1995, p. 63). The term "co-transference" speaks to the inseparability of transference and countertransference. The main theoretical concept of Orange, Atwood, and Stolorow (1997) is that of "organizing principles," *emotional convictions developed through relational experiences in one's childhood.* Fundamental to this theory is the idea that organizing principles of therapist and patient overlap; there is an intersection of subjectivities. These organizing principles interact by

---

[19] The term "co-transference" (Bradway, 1991, Bradway & McCoard, 1997) is also frequently used in sandplay. It seems that Bradway coined the term first. Her conceptualization of "co-transference" will be elaborated further in the next section.

way of "reciprocal, mutual influence," which seems to replace the concept of projective identification[20] used in other theories. The goal of therapy is to increase the flexibility of the patient's organizing principles, as they become more available to conscious reflection. Orange, Atwood and Stolorow (1997) also debunk the notion of the "neutral analyst," and state that transference and countertransference are always expressions of the unconscious organizing activity of both.

Aron (1996), Orange (1995), Ogden (1994) and Orange, Atwood and Stolorow (1997) describe similar notions of mutual creation by therapist and client of the intersubjective field, based on the unconscious experience of the participants and their related emotional convictions. These descriptions of the field reflect generally accepted current theory. They address the subtleties of both the background and the foreground of the interaction within the therapeutic dyad. It seems that most contemporary writers, with the exception of Stolorow, Orange and Atwood (1997), agree that a non-pathologizing version of projective identification is necessary to really convey how visceral and powerful the experience of unconscious communication may be, and to invite and allow the clinician to empathically understand that communication. For most psychoanalytic theorists, projective identification is acknowledged as an interpersonal experience in everyday life, not just in the psychotherapeutic hour.

Conclusion

Stephen Mitchell (1997), one of the most prolific writers on relational theory, states, "Countertransference, like the weather, continually changes, but one is never without it" (p. 182). Countertransference has often been thought of as a storm from which one periodically emerges, but the current view is that countertransference is always there. When it has a benign quality, we simply may not notice it. This is similar to Ogden's (1994) view of transference/countertransference as background music, and Aron's (1996) view of enactments and projective identification as a continual process. The use of countertransference is now thought of as

---

[20] Stolorow (Stolorow, Orange, & Atwood, 1997) is adamantly opposed to the concept of projective identification. Rather, he speaks of *mutual, reciprocal influence.*

a primary tool in psychoanalytic theory, in which meaning is arrived at through a "meeting of minds" (Aron, 1996, p. xii).

I believe that these two points — that countertransference is always there, and that full attunement to the therapist's own subjective experience can be a barometer for understanding both the client's experience and the symbolic field — are important additions for sandplay theory. But before I examine sandplay countertransference theory in light of these developments, I will briefly address transference/countertransference phenomena in trauma work because it is with early trauma that sandplay therapy does some of its most important work, and it is in this arena that we encounter some of our most difficult countertransference experiences.

Chapter 4

Countertransference in Trauma Work

Here we find words being used in place of action —
as weapons, as camouflage, as a desperate cry for help,
a cry of rage or of any other intense emotional state
of which the patient is but dimly aware. These feeling states
may have no connection with what the patient is recounting.

— Joyce McDougall, 1993

Trauma, as I am using the concept, includes the resulting deficits. I will define trauma in the same way as Donald Kalsched (1996), to mean

> any experience that causes the child unbearable psychic pain or anxiety. For an experience to be 'unbearable' means that it overwhelms the usual defensive measures which Freud (1920b: 27) described as a 'protective shield against stimuli.' Trauma of this magnitude varies from the acute, shattering experiences of child abuse so prominent in the literature today to the more 'cumulative traumas' of unmet dependency-needs that mount up to devastating effect in some children's development (Khan, 1963).

> These include the more acute deprivations of infancy described by Winnicott as 'primitive agonies', the experience of which is 'unthinkable' (1963: 90). The distinguishing feature of such trauma is what Heinz Kohut (1977: 104) called 'disintegration anxiety', an unnameable dread associated with the threatened dissolution of a coherent self. (p. 1)

It is in our work with trauma that clinicians may encounter some of our most difficult relational experiences. Psychologist Constance J. Dalenberg (2000), exploring the vicissitudes of the countertransference in trauma work, writes that it is difficult to work with trauma patients because it is difficult to manage our own intense reactions, and therefore difficult to provide safety. There is frequently an intense, life-and-death quality to the transference/countertransference that can take over the therapist.

Yet, a traumatized client needs a more reliable emotional environment than other clients because "attachment-related surprise" is more frightening than it might be for others (Dalenberg, 2000, p. 31). It is the potential triggering of the therapist's countertransference acting out of feelings of disapproval, disgust, or rejection that feels unsafe, particularly to the traumatized client. Often in work with traumatized patients, the therapist will experience a complementary countertransference by being placed in the role of abuser to the client's victim. Creating a safe environment — although making it feel completely safe is never really possible — necessitates attention to the *actual* countertransference of the therapist and to the *expected* countertransference from the client's perspective (Dalenberg, 2000).

The traumatized client may attack or accuse the therapist in an effort at self-protection, arousing the therapist's defenses. Client ambivalence regarding attachment may feel exhausting to the therapist. For these reasons, and given the intensity of the field, the therapist may feel shame over her sense of inadequacy in facing such tremendous pain. Yet, this shame is frequently denied. Countertransference shame may come from many sources, such as the therapist's unacceptable feelings and limitations or from an enhanced awareness of the harshness and cruelty of the world (Dalenberg, 2000). In an attempt to deny the shame, the therapist may unknowingly withdraw her empathy, or unknowingly regress and empathically merge with the client. Dalenberg (2000) makes it clear that countertransference experiences must be *felt* by the therapist in order to provide optimal safety. She states that "felt compassion allows for safe emergence of traumatic material," and quotes Jung: "You can exert no influence if you are not susceptible to influence (as cited in Dalenberg, 2000, p. 241). Dalenberg's views seem to agree with Dora Kalff's (1980) view (explored in the next section) that safety is paramount. However, Dalenberg describes a way of providing a free and protected space through attentiveness to the fluctuations and deep feelings in the countertransference.

French psychoanalyst Joyce McDougall (1993) describes "meaningless communication" taking place in trauma therapy. She points to the countertransference experience of feeling invaded and rendered useless *because the experience does not seem to be related to content.* This mirrors Goodheart's (1980) *persona-restoring* field, the out-of-contact field, the field of the merger transference. In this field, language becomes an act rather than a means to communicate. This may make for a confusing and unsettling countertransference experience because the client's evacuation of disturbing feelings can result in a countertransference of blankness. Yet, this way of communicating has a purpose. Speech becomes an attempt to make the analyst *experience* something. Meaning therefore can only be captured in the countertransference experience within the body of the therapist. This form of communication results from traumas that affect the patient's capacity to self-reflect and to contain and actually feel painful emotions.

McDougall (1993) explains the primary importance of being in relationship with, or being connected to the Other:

> This vital link to the Other may override in importance the symbolic function which consists of the desire to *inform* someone of something. From such a viewpoint verbal communications might be considered an approximation to crying, calling out, screaming, growling rather than to *telling* something. (p. 287-288)

> Fusional communion, that archaic form of loving which is the nursling's right, is still implicitly awaited by certain adults. (p. 291)

For the client, this is both a way of remaining in intimate connection and also of conveying and discharging emotion directly with the intent to affect and arouse the Other, both appealing for help and pushing the analyst away at the same time. This is an attempt to share a pain which could not yet be expressed through language and could not yet be *thought* about or consciously *felt*.

McDougall (1993) describes how the analyst is likely to feel bewildered and invaded by such experiences unless he pays attention to them. This fusional communication is "a demand to be *heard rather than listened to;* a need for communion rather than communication" (p. 289). "The demand to be understood without words implies a terror of facing disappointment or refusal of any kind," which is felt as "an unbearable pain ... which may destroy one" (p. 291). "Psychic suffering at this presymbolic phase is indistinguishable from physical suffering" (p. 271) —a suffering that has no words, and that makes it unsafe to trust another with one's vulnerability.

McDougall (1993) says that we may think of this as the need to use others as containers for unbearable affect (Bion, 1963/1977), or the urgent need to recover lost parts of the self through selfobjects (Kohut, 1971, 1977). This form of communication seeks to restore the primary mother-child unity and its potential for soothing by "experiencing through the other" (Sands, 1997a). Often the analyst will feel that he is unable to function adequately with a particular client, and yet it is the task of the analyst to "decode the sounds of distress" (McDougall, 1993, p. 299), to provide a "mindwomb" (Wrye, 2001) that can think for the client until the client is able to think for himself.

McDougall (1993) seems to disagree with Goodheart's (1980) assessment of how to work in this field. Contrary to Goodheart, she tells us that an attitude of "expectant silence" generates isolation and hopelessness to these clients: "their need to feel that they exist in other people's eyes, to feel truly alive, to a large degree dominates all other wishes, and invades almost totally the territory of desire" (p. 302). The intervention here is not silence, nor interpretation, but creating potentially vital space for the feelings and thoughts to come into being. This *space* may be found in the mind and body of the therapist.

In Dalenburg's and McDougall's descriptions of countertransference in trauma work, we may recognize Goodheart's (1980) "persona-restoring" and "complex-discharging" fields (Goodheart, 1980). The elucidation of their dangers and meanings by Dalenberg (2000) and McDougall (1993) provides theoretical ground for sandplay theory, which does not yet formally acknowledge any field other than the *secured-symbolizing* field. I believe this limits sandplay therapy, because many clients bring to us their nonverbal trauma in the form of these other two fields. These clients use sandplay in a way that is not yet explainable according to existing sandplay theory, because their sandplay work does not occur in the transitional space or the unconscious alignment — the "feeling with" — of the co-transference. I will further explore this idea in Part III where I describe four qualities of relatedness. But, first, let us look at countertransference from neuroscience and attachment points of view.

Chapter 5

Countertransference in Neuroscience and Attachment Theory

The roots of resilience lie in the sense of being understood by, and existing in, the mind and the heart of a loving, attuned, self-possessed Other.

— *Diana Fosha*

The repair of early attachment injuries and the healing of unrelatedness from within the clinical relationship are now seen as our main tasks as depth therapists. Relatedness is crucial in understanding both the neurobiological and psychic dimensions of human growth and change. Emerging energies between client and therapist, like warp and weft, weave new patterns of interrelatedness and repair old ones. In this process, we actually co-create new neural pathways in the brain. Neuroscience and attachment research have now actually validated the healing value of the clinical approaches presented in Chapters 1-4.

Sullivan (2010) notes that *relatedness* refers to something as fundamental as the air we breathe. We begin life in relatedness, and we grow into who we are through the various qualities of relationship we encounter. As the social creatures that we are, we are forever embedded in relatedness.

Sullivan explains that the roots of the word *relate* lie in the idea of coming "back, again" together with "suffering" and "bearing." "Relationship implies that two substances have been brought back together after being separated ... When we are in relationship to another, parts of ourselves that we have lost touch with are carried back into connection with us" (p. 8). Being *related* includes recognizing our similarities to the other, and suffering arises as we are brought back to ourselves to face disowned shadow aspects. It is within relationship that we may discover that the wounds of the other may also exist in ourselves. This is usually a painful experience. Indeed, relatedness both "hurts" and "nourishes" (p. 8). These are profound insights into the human needs and fears held within the archetypes of attachment and relationship.

As we strive for a deep sensitivity to the conscious and unconscious energies manifesting in the relational field, including those given form in an image, we may focus on the relational energies that nourish, rather than those that hurt. By "hurting" I mean such things as empathic failures by the therapist (this hurts the client), complementary identifications or resonance with bad internal objects (this hurts both), or the hurting involved in holding deep despair, resistance, trauma or violent images (this may "hurt" the therapist). I would like to explore the idea that "hurting" is inherent in relatedness, and when these energies arise, they have deep relational meanings and tremendous therapeutic potential. Work in the countertransference embodies both the difficulties and the nourishment of being related. Difficult countertransference experiences, and the "hurting" of being more consciously related, are fertile ground in the relational field, ripe with precious information.

Positive Emotional Experience

We have always understood that in sandplay, the subjective experience of the therapist would be — should be — that of loving, compassionate holding accompanied by feelings of interest, curiosity, and joy as we empathically participate in the sandplayer's experience. It is generally accepted that the countertransference container must be one of unconditional positive regard and warmth.

54

Neuroscience confirms what sandplay therapists have long known: a surround of rapport and positive emotional experience is absolutely essential in healing. Positive transference and emotional safety are necessary to actually transform negative, entrenched emotional-relational patterns in the brain (Schore, 2003).

Equally important however is attachment theory's emphasis on our own sensitivity in attending to the whole of our own — and our clients' — subjective experience (Wallin, 2007), particularly when this experience is negative.

Facilitating Secure Attachment

Attachment research indicates that a parent's *inclusive attunement* to the child's full range of subjective experience facilitates secure attachment. Affect that is welcomed in this way becomes integrated in the child; affect that is not accepted or acknowledged, for whatever reason, becomes traumatically walled off, disavowed, and unavailable for conscious reflection or verbalization (Wallin, 2007).

A child will integrate only those experiences that her primary caregivers can accept and hold, and will exclude from awareness those thoughts, feelings, and behaviors that might disrupt her most crucial attachment relationships. These unacceptable experiences then remain undeveloped, unintegrated, and impossible to verbalize. They become the *unthought known* (Bollas, 1987) — nearly unreachable places in the psyche that hold implicit experiences of relational trauma. Neuroscience is discovering how these walled off experiences may land in raw form in the body of the therapist, and may thereby become, for the first time, integrated and known. This integration of split off trauma can happen *even as the therapist remains silent* while attending to her reverie.

Implicit Relational Knowing: Right Brain-to-Right Brain

As noted earlier, relationship is now considered the key factor in the creation of the structure and functioning of the brain, as well as the formation of relational patterns in the mind. Neuroscience tells us that *relationship is a pattern of energy exchange over time* (Siegel, 1999). One way this energy exchange happens is through right brain-to-right brain communication (Schore, 2003).

The right brain is the seat of the implicit self, or what we might call the unconscious mind. It participates in *nonrational* experience, including experiences of trauma as well as empathy and trust. *The right brain communicates its unconscious states to other right brains that are attuned to receive these communications.* This kind of communication happens constantly, nonverbally, implicitly (Schore, 2003).

Neuroscience finds that these right brain-to-right brain communications regulate affect not only in the mother-infant dyad, but in the therapist-client dyad as well. *Right brain-to-right brain communication is also the form of communication experienced in the countertransference* (Schore, 2003). The right brain of the therapist receives and decodes the nonverbal communications from the client through empathically resonating with *her own* actual felt, somatic reactions. This form of communication — this silent, somatic-emotional conversation in the matriarchal unconscious — conveys the *unthought known* of presymbolic states to the therapist. In this way, preverbal trauma is communicated between client and therapist right brain-to-right brain, without words.

The Unthought Known

Preverbal experience lives at the sensory, somatic core of the self and this kind of experience is communicated implicitly, somatically and without words (Wallin, 2007). We sense this: at times, we may have an intuitive sense, a bodily knowing, an experience of the visceral, affective state of the other that we cannot always articulate. This is our experience of the *unthought known* (Bollas, 1987): that which has always been known, but has never really been *available* to be felt or thought about. It is therefore an unconscious or unintegrated knowing, an implicit knowing. It represents the same psychic territory that McDougall (1994) describes (see Chapter 4), in which intolerable preverbal experiences are not yet accessible to thought or words, and may be experienced by the therapist in her countertransference.

Research advises us to *embody* and *feel into* our own confusion, uncertainty, and doubt (Wallin, 2007). *This embodiment in the therapist facilitates change in the area of the client's brain that transforms a bodily felt sense into a subjectively felt emotion* (Schore, 2003). This transformation is from pre-symbolic to symbolic, from unthought known to that which can be thought about and felt. It is the transformation of preverbal trauma from implicit to explicit knowing as it becomes held, contained and integrated.

The unthought known is communicated through the transference/ countertransference, right brain-to-right brain. Many theorists feel that this is where we find the greatest potential for therapeutic change (Wallin, 2007), and that we need to make room for the reverberation of all affects and states of mind within ourselves and eventually come to symbolic understanding of them. To be therapeutic, the therapist needs to listen with her own body — somatically, emotionally, and relationally — to what is communicated nonverbally, to hear and come to understand the disguised nonverbal communication of the patient.

I have been fascinated to discover that research in neuroscience and attachment theory lends support to contemporary analytic ideas about clinical process. Clinical experience has shown us that these silent yet often disturbing communications through the therapist's countertransference sometimes may be the *only* way for severely traumatized persons to communicate their preverbal distress (Dalenberg, 2000; Wallin, 2007). The unthought known may come into awareness as a niggling intuition or the equivalent of a silent scream that we recognize in our own experience of the relational field. This happens when we are vaguely troubled by not being able to think about or consciously feel or make sense of the session. The unthought known, tugging at our unconscious, insists on its need to be there. There are several ways in which we might understand this phenomenon.

Contemporary models of working therapeutically with countertransference encourage us to attend to the deeply unconscious, symbolic meanings of any negative subjective experience and to continuously "come back" into connection with the Other through loving relationship with our own disowned parts (see Racker, Chapter 1). Scientific, theoretical and clinical guidelines point to consciously using our countertransference experience by applying something like *mindfulness* to our own complementary countertransference.

Mindfulness

Mindfulness is a quality of awareness that emerges through deliberate and nonjudgmental attention to the unfolding of experience, moment by moment (Kabat-Zinn, 2005). Mindfulness is compassionate attunement with the self, resulting in noticing what is occurring in the present moment without judgment. Mindfulness requires suspending memory and desire, and it also requires self-reflection (Wallin, 2007). Through mindfulness, we scan our bodymind, feeling into the nuances of our somatic-emotional experience, thereby gradually gaining access to the unthought known. This new level of understanding is conveyed to the client through right brain-to-right brain communication and sometimes through words. Mindfulness in the therapist can actually facilitate a relationship with the patient that builds his self-reflection and, eventually, earned secure attachment (Wallin, 2007).

Part II

Transference/Countertransference in Sandplay:
Expanding and Deepening the Free and Protected Space

On the other hand, as we have already seen, the therapist/counselor
must be capable of establishing a free and protected space.
What we want to mediate for others should emerge
from our own experience. This means that the therapist/counselor
should possess an openness that is the fruit of an open encounter
with one's own dark and unknown sides.

— Dora Kalff, 1991

In Part II, I explore the theory of sandplay's treatment of the clinical relationship and the positive aura that surrounds it. There is an implicit emphasis on protective feelings in the countertransference. And although it is slowly changing, for most of sandplay's history the more difficult relational experiences are not really addressed. I will explore some possible reasons for this, and then, using the ideas about unconscious communication described in Part I, attempt to expand and deepen our capacities for holding in the free and protected space, following Kalff's guidance regarding the "open encounter with one's own dark and unknown sides."

Chapter 6

Exploring Sandplay's Emphasis on Positive Transference/ Countertransference

I aim to give the child's Self the possibility of constellating and manifesting itself in therapy. And I try, through the transference, to protect it and to stabilize the relationship between the Self and the ego.

— *Dora Kalff, 1980*

There is actually very little written about the therapist's subjective experience of the clinical relationship in sandplay. Most published cases have focused on the symbolic meaning as visible in the tray.

There are many possible reasons for this, including Kalff's understanding of transference as protection and safety; a subsequent idealization of the positive Mother; a limited definition of *containment* within the free and protected space; the emphasis on empathic immersion; and the inherent protective function of the sand tray itself.

Transference/Countertransference as Protection and Safety

As the originator of Jungian sandplay, Kalff (1980) has a profound effect on the conceptualization, if not our actual experience, of transference and countertransference in sandplay. Because of her understanding of transference on the part of the therapist as a source of protection for the client, transference in sandplay is almost exclusively understood to be a positive, protected experience. Bradway and McCoard (1997) explain:

> The term "transference," as used by Dora Kalff, refers primarily to the "free and protected space" which is the hallmark of her therapy. In the introduction to her book, she says that she tries through the transference to "protect" the child's Self when it is constellated in the therapy. (p. 31)

For Kalff (1980), transference/countertransference in sandplay means the general positive relationship between therapist and client, based on promoting the client's experience of safety and trust. In this sense, Kalff seems to equate transference with the therapeutic alliance. She explains that the transference experience needs to be positive in order to enhance the possibility for the constellation of the Self, which for her is the primary goal of a sandplay process, because it is the constellation of the Self that marks the moment of deepest healing and transformation.[21]

Kalff (1980) never says that the therapist will feel only positive feelings with regard to her clients, yet this is implied in the way she writes about her own experiences and in her use of the word transference to indicate the free and protected space. This positive experience that occurs within a positive transference is understood to heal the rupture in the mother-child

---

[21] Cameron (2003), in an exploration of the appearance of the Self in sandplay therapy, explains: "Sandplay therapy seeks to restore damage to the ego-Self connection by creating the conditions for the ego to experience the Self" (p. 133). "A shift occurs within the sandplayer and the sandplay process when the Self appears. There is a coalescence, a connection and a release of energy within the sandplayer. A Self experience is associated with a culmination, an integration and an ordering of the elements of the sandplayer's unfolding issues or story. The deep internal connection and shift that the sandplayer experiences when the Self appears, releases psychic energy that may be used for the transformation of the personality" (p. 135).

unity and to aid in the constellation of the Self. She writes, "This free space occurs in the therapeutic situation when the therapist is able to accept the child fully ..." (p. 30). Weinrib (1983) elaborates:

> Sandplay therapy provides the conditions for a womb-like incubatory period that makes possible the repair of a damaged mother-image which, in turn, enables *constellation* and activation of the Self. (p. 2)

For Kalff (1980), the constellation of the Self "... is the most important moment in the development of the personality" (p. 29). The constellation of the Self in sandplay is recognized primarily by the numinous experience that accompanies it, an experience that is highly valued by sandplay therapists. Amatruda and Helm Simpson (1997) provide an exquisite description of this experience:

> Witnessing a Self tray is a deeply moving experience. The energy in the therapy room brightens. The client and therapist are enlivened. There is often a tingling up and down the spine that happens in the presence of spirit, truth and new birth. The air shimmers. (p. 87)

Based on the necessity of recreating the oneness or merger experience of the mother-child unity to make possible the constellation of the Self, Kalff's understanding of the *transference as protection* becomes clear. This theoretical position is based on the developmental theory of Neumann (1973), who identifies three phases of development that Kalff felt exemplified the sandplay process. The first stage is the uroboric stage of mother-child unity, in which the mother is the infant's entire world and carries the Self for it. In the second stage, the infant's Self detaches from and is in relationship with the mother; and, in the third, the Self is constellated within the child, establishing a sense of basic trust.[22]

While Neumann's (1973) model provides the foundation of Kalff's developmental theory, there is also another Jungian model used by some

---

[22] This is just like Winnicott's complete dependence in the mother-infant mind; transitional space, the necessary ground for beginning individuation from the mother; and then the capacity for "use of the object" allowing the child's independence to come into being (Patricia Marra, personal communication, January 15, 2013).

sandplay therapists, that articulates and explains the negative and positive vicissitudes of the transference/countertransference experience (Donelan, 1999). The developmental school of Jungian analyst Michael Fordham (1957/1974) understands the constellation of the Self in a slightly different way, as a process of continuous *deintegration* and *reintegration*, resulting in the building of ego. This is a process of containment and metabolization of primitive experience by the (m)Other, and explicitly involves the full range of felt countertransference experience in the mother/therapist. In many sandplay processes, the continuing deintegration and reintegration is visible as fragmentation and cohesiveness alternate from one tray to the next, even after the occurrence of a Self tray. As mentioned in Chapter 2, Fordham emphasizes the therapeutic importance of the therapist's *deintegrating* — opening herself up to and embodying — the visceral and emotional experience of the relational field.

In Fordham's (1957/1974) more detailed view, the constellation of the Self is not only a single moment in the development of the personality, but a potentially recurring event throughout one's lifetime. The individual must go through these sometimes painful de-integrative experiences again and again. However, once the initial constellation of the Self has occurred, a living connection with the unconscious makes this a more conscious and meaningful process. The views of Fordham and Kalff may seem to be in conflict, and yet, paradoxically, both are clinically relevant, and both hold emotional and experiential truth for the sandplay therapist. In fact, holding both theories in our sandplay work may help us to better work within the wholeness of the Mother archetype.

Idealization of the Positive Mother

Kalff's (1980) theoretical position regarding the importance of the constellation of the Self may be an important influence for the implied positive countertransference in the sandplay literature. It explains her commitment to constellating the accepting, nurturing pole of the mother archetype within the therapeutic relationship. In development, we would all hope for an ideal, loving, securely attached mother who could easily digest our intolerable sensory and emotional experiences, fluently giving meaning to them. And yet so many of our clients come to us because they have not had this quality of attunement, and they bring with them the vicissitudes of their early relational trauma.

In our clinical work, consistency, reliability, warmth, and acceptance are paramount in creating the safe holding environment. It is through the non-interpretive, emotionally reliable backdrop of holding that deeply injured clients may develop a "cocoon transference" (Slochower, 1991, p. 710; 1996) in which they experience early ego states, eventually feeling safe enough to allow affective experience to become more conscious.

Sandplay focuses on the early mothering stage, which ideally is a stage of harmonious union. When this early union has not been optimal, patients may symbolically regress in the sand to birth, conception, or even earlier in an effort to repair early trauma. In this regression the therapist may experience empathic resonance with the client's early experiences of mis-attunement, and this resonance may be painful.

Mutual positive mirroring and positive transference/countertransference are necessary in the "oneness" phases of early attachment. However, even in a state of oneness — such as with a primitive idealizing transference — a positive experience for the client can still be a difficult experience for the therapist, particularly in the verbal part of a therapy. Therapists often remark that when involved in this kind of a merger transference/countertransference, they feel like they don't exist, or they feel controlled or "taken over." Even with the use of the sand, preverbal trauma may arise in this way within the free and protected space. This an opportunity for it to be witnessed, felt, metabolized, and healed.

Developmentally, there is a stage in which it is necessary for the child to be able to look up to a special person as an ideal of strength and perfection. This is soothing for the child (Kohut, 1971, 1977) and eventually becomes part of his or her self structure as the ability to self-soothe. An idealizing transference is developmentally necessary when an initial idealizing experience with a powerful, soothing other is missing in one's life. Given a free and protected space, particular unmet developmental needs will arise in the transference/countertransference field. The therapist need not attempt to artificially create a positive internal experience, nor transcend a negative one, but must be able to fully reside in whatever quality the field holds.

All of this can happen within the loving psychic embrace of unconditional positive regard and love. One problem with the understanding of the transference/countertransference solely as protection and positive feeling is that there may be a very subtle quality of omnipotence or superiority expected of the sandplay therapist. This could even lead to an unconscious "inflated" stance — a countertransference attempt to rise above these negative experiences which beg not for transcendence but for digestion, not for an airy *sublimatio*, but for a grounded, solid, integrated *coagulatio*.

To assume that the therapist can protect the client from negative experience and make her feel completely safe at the level of the unconscious is unrealistic, particularly in working with any kind of trauma. To imagine that we can have real relationship without negative feelings such as envy, anger, shame, or rage is a wish that rejects our own anxieties and primitive needs. Clinging only to the positive pole of the Mother archetype may actually diminish the free and protected space. This view virtually eliminates the shadow of the therapist in sandplay, especially if we consider Racker's concept of complementary countertransference, in which the therapist symbolically may become — both in the client's eyes and in the therapist's own experience — a reflection of the bad internal object.

This shadow material may be difficult for sandplay therapists to hold if we are drawn to the all-good pole of the Mother archetype. Because of needs arising from our own early experiences, we may not only embrace this one-sided, all-good image, but identify with it, perhaps out of our own desire to mother or to be mothered in this ideal way. In order to tolerate negative countertransference experiences, we need to have integrated "an open encounter with [our] own dark and unknown sides" (Kalff, 1991).

A Closer Look at the Free and Protected Space

Kalff's theory emphasizes a positive therapeutic relationship built on safety, acceptance and trust. This is, of course, the foundation of any good therapy, and, as previously stated, this need for a positive transference in order to constellate healing is confirmed by neuroscience.

I believe that Kalff's (1980) conception of the "free and protected space" was originally intended to help the therapist hold *everything*.

66

But it may in fact have the opposite effect of diminishing awareness of our negative subjective experiences. We need to look at other theories to find an emphasis on the therapeutic use of negative countertransference experiences.

Jung (1946/1966) makes it clear that *transference is something the therapist neither intentionally elicits nor controls.* Within the holding environment of safety and acceptance, negative feelings and experiences often arise and need to be contained — worked with internally — by the therapist. These experiences *need* to arise, so that they can be mediated by another human being. We need to provide ample space within ourselves to metabolize and humanize the *archetypal affects* of terror, anguish, rage, shame, and contempt in psychotherapy, as well as joy, interest, and surprise (Stewart, 1987).

For this, we really need to consider *containment* — that which happens *inside* the therapist. This concept could be a valuable addition to sandplay theory. It is alluded to by Ammann (1991): "We can experience this body consciousness in an intimate love relationship or in the early mother-child relationship when this very subtle, nonverbal, non-imagistic exchange of bodily energies takes place" (p. 26).

It is frequently stated in the literature that sandplay is particularly effective in cases of maternal deprivation, or ruptures in the mother-child unity. This deprivation is related to the unmet need for transformation of raw archetypal, instinctual experience into tolerable, usable, namable emotions. This, according to Bion (1963/1977), happens in the mother/therapist as container. In Bion's model, *uncontainable anxieties* are "placed" into the containing mother by the infant through projective identification. Containment happens through the mother's reverie and attending to her own internal experience of strong or subtle inchoate affects and musings, coming to understand them with her body and mind, and then "returning" them to her infant, but now transformed by the understanding that symbolic meaning gives to these anxieties. The experience of containment may not always be a positive subjective experience for the "container." In fact, Bion speaks of the container's "dread" of the contained material. Sandplay theory is only now beginning to address the possibility of the body and mind of the therapist viscerally being taken over, and the therapist then containing and returning this raw archetypal experience in mediated form. In the words of Mitrani (2001):

> As one can readily see, the ability to 'contain' assumes a mother who has boundaries and sufficient internal space to accommodate her own anxieties as well as those acquired in relation to her infant; a mother who has a well-developed capacity to bear pain, to contemplate, to think and to convey what she thinks *in a way that is meaningful to her infant.* (p. 1091)

Containing is a concept that includes, but goes beyond, a loving provision of free and protected space, to include the discovery of silent interpretation, including the therapist's internal thinking, feeling, reverie and eventual symbolizing. Neuroscience has confirmed that this *silent interpretation* is communicated, between the right brains of therapist and client, and is deeply healing.

The transference — particularly with a traumatized client — may not feel completely "safe" to the client for a long, long time, particularly at unconscious levels when one has experienced early relational trauma. This feeling of being somehow unsafe will likely in some way be experienced in the countertransference. In contemporary analytic theory, the transference is never inherently "safe" — it simply is an experience based on the shared unconscious of the two unique persons who are emotionally engaging within the field. The fundamental importance of the free and protected space does not at all eliminate the therapist's need to attend to all of her experience and feelings — positive as well as negative.

Empathic Immersion

Empathic immersion is one of our most important tools in psychotherapy. Its healing powers are well known. And yet emphasis on empathic immersion with the client, the sand picture, and the visual symbol may inadvertently minimize the therapist's awareness of her own self-experience. It seems that both the sandplay literature and the sandplay work itself evoke this immersion into the client's experience.

Sandplay therapists enter into the sandworld — the client's internal world as it manifests in that moment within the clinical relationship — and are captivated by it. We can't help it. We experience that world empathically, putting ourselves in the shoes of the client, but often stepping out of our own shoes completely. Perhaps because of the theoretical and experiential emphasis on the sandworld and on the internal world of the client, most writers on sandplay do not discuss their own associations, bodily sensations, intense feelings, memories, or reveries, although thoughts and softer feelings regarding sandtrays are sometimes mentioned in the literature.

By focusing on the tray and the subjective world of the client, sandplay therapists take the "empathic vantage point" (Kohut, 1959, 1971, 1977, 1984) of self psychology. As Sands (1997a) points out, "the emphasis on immersing ourselves in the patient's experience cannot help but minimize the importance of the analyst's experience" (p. 659). Sands makes another important point about the empathic stance that also applies to sandplay, stating that the theory

> suggests that we can deliberately assume a particular vantage point, an empathic one, and that we really can determine what the patient's experience is, as distinct from our own. It assumes a separateness that is in fact not always there. (p. 659)

Because, at a deeper level, we are not really that separate, it is helpful to look to our own subjective experience as well as the client's to deepen our empathic resonance in the relational field.

The Protective Function of the Sandtray

Another possible reason for the emphasis on positive transference/countertransference is found in the inherent protective function of the sandtray. Through sandplay, the client can reveal traumatic aspects of her experience symbolically while sometimes protecting both members of the dyad from the horror of direct re-experiencing of trauma. Bradway and McCoard (1997) discuss how the positive transference/countertransference may be safeguarded by the sand picture itself: it is easier to tolerate transference and countertransference when played out in the tray, rather than in the self of the therapist. Many believe that in sandplay, where the negative material may be presented in the tray, it is not as likely to affect the client-therapist relationship as it does in verbal therapy (Donelan, 1999; Bradway & McCoard, 1997; Bradway, 1991).

There are at least three implications of this view. First, difficult feelings may sometimes be held by the symbolic elements in the tray rather than in the self of the therapist. It is the nature of the symbol to unite the opposites and to hold both obvious and unknown meanings. When a symbol is placed in the sand, it is a symbol of both the wound and the healing, in one moment. When negative affect is revealed in a symbol, the positive is also reflected; the image holding the affect may protect the therapist from the full force of negative feelings. Thus the sandplay itself may help to provide a metabolizing function for difficult feelings (Cunningham, 1997). The concretizing of even extremely painful emotions can bring relief to the therapist. Ammann's (1991) case of "Eva" describes an arduous countertransference; yet Ammann says:

> ... without [the sand pictures] I wonder if I could have marshalled the strength and patience to carry on this extraordinarily difficult therapy ... certain sand pictures of my analysands become a source of strength to me. (p. 57)

Second, the sand itself appears to have a calming effect. One way to think about this is that the client is metaphorically working in the body of the therapist.[23] We know from neuroscience that there is a physical, body-to-body co-regulation that happens in the therapeutic dyad, and the therapist's body provides affect regulation. With the use of the sandtray, we have the added metaphorical "working in the body of the mother" that provides an intimate calming experience. Working in the sand may actually help clients who felt uncontained as infants experience containment through re-experiencing their own bodily edges, while simultaneously being contained by the therapist. As we imagine this, we hold image and relational experience together.

---

[23] Cynthia O'Connell, personal communication, April 27, 2001

I have had experiences in which I felt soothed by my client's work in the sand, or in which the client became immediately calm with the use of the sandtray. Anxiety seemed to melt into the sand itself. At other times, I have had the experience of clients happily working in the sand while I felt surges of panic in my body, clearly related to my clients' earlier traumatic experiences. And I have had many experiences wherein my clients with preverbal trauma, through our long work both in verbal and sandplay therapy, found their own edges, experienced containment, and slowly developed the capacity to self-soothe.

Third, the sandtray itself may function as a "bastion" for the work — a protected interpersonal area with clearly defined boundaries that is not available at the moment for transformation in the therapeutic relationship. And just as the tray may serve as a bastion, the therapist, too, may function in this way, unconsciously titrating the awareness of traumatic feelings or experiences. Residing in the therapist's countertransference, this walled off place may sometimes be identified by a "not feeling" in the therapist — a countertransference experience of blankness or unthought known, and is not necessarily a hindrance to the therapy unless it remains unrecognized. It may represent a pacing mechanism, allowing negative and potentially destructive material a chance to lie low, slowly metabolizing or waiting to reveal itself until there is enough safety within the relationship.

These are profound possibilities for the ways in which sandplay can hold some things that a given therapist/client pair could not easily hold interpersonally. However they are also statements that may speak to the limits of the sandplay method, especially if it is relied on without an active use of the therapist's subjective experience.

Donelan (1999) finds that sandplay therapists agree that the transference is somewhat "masked" in the symbols and that, in fact, the sandtray may be used defensively in this way. For clients who are as yet unable to work more consciously with relational issues evoked in the therapy, the sandtray may function as a protected place where this material may be both concealed and revealed. Yet, it is important for the therapist to look for indications of transference in the sandtray because the synchronistic moment — that moment when "the presentation of the unconscious by the patient in the

sandtray and the simultaneous recognition of it as such by the therapist"
— is deeply healing (Kalff, 1975, in Bradway and McCoard, 1997, p. 85).

If the transference/countertransference, or total situation, of the
relational field is also experienced in the mindwomb of the therapist,
these bastions or masked places in the psyche may become even more
available for healing. Mitchell and Friedman (1994) begin to address
this when they write:

> ... a therapist may experience feelings of incongruence when
> watching a client make a "pretty" tray while experiencing it as
> superficial... *The reality of these feelings needs to be included in
> the understanding of the tray.* (p. 86, Italics mine)

Barren trays or "pretty trays" may represent a bastion in that they represent
a reaching out, a longing for *contact with* — and simultaneously a desperate
need for *protection from* — the therapist. In this way, the sandplay may be
used in an indirect way to make contact (Miller, 1979), protecting the
client's deep vulnerabilities.

An aspect of the uniqueness of sandplay lies in its visual, sensate
quality (Donelan, 1999). Given the fact that the transference/
countertransference is often visible in the tray extends this uniqueness.
However, the assumption that because sandplay is visual, the transference/
countertransference will be seen solely with the eyes is only half correct.
The visual aspect is, of course, important; this gives us an additional means
of apprehending the client's experience. Yet, there is so much more. The
transference/countertransference field holds, supports, and facilitates the
transformation that is visible in the sand, and at the same time it informs
the therapist of the client's vital inner reality.

Chapter 7

Evidence for A Full Range of Countertransference Experience

[Milner (1987)] associates analytic openness with pregnant emptiness, creative darkness, the power of non-existence, the goodness of absolute vacuity, the matrix of the sense of self, the divine ground of one's being, the experience of breathing.

— *Michael Eigen, 1998*

Relational issues frequently appear symbolically in the sandtray, arising from the client's implicit memories and relational patterns. In sandplay, the transference/countertransference is sometimes safeguarded or masked, and the therapist may be sheltered from directly receiving the client's negative feelings. Even so, a few early examples exist in the sandplay literature of the therapist's deep resonance with negative affect in the relational field, which I've included at the end of this chapter.

I found in my interviews with seasoned sandplay therapists that their subjective experience includes a full range of positive and negative experience, held within the transpersonal container of the archetypal transference/countertransference (Cunningham, 2003). Following is a summary of what I learned.

Research on The Subjective Experience of the Sandplay Therapist

The subjective experience of the sandplay therapist is vividly alive, encompassing a wide range of human experiential states — positive and negative, ineffable and extraordinary. The initial and sometimes general countertransference experience is described as delightful, pleasurable, focused and fully present, poignant and mysterious.

The transference/countertransference matrix of sandplay is full of human emotion, experiential states, intuitions, visceral bodily experiences, and thinking, and, to a lesser extent, reverie, fantasy, memories, dreams, and images. These experiences may be deeply uncomfortable, disturbing, or almost unbearable for the therapist, or, at the other extreme, they may be joyful or transcendent. This full range of subjective experience includes countertransference to particular figures or constellations of figures, to particular trays or series of trays, to particular clients, and to the unique quality of the relational field that holds the work in the sand.

The Initial and Often General Experience of the Sandplay Therapist: Pleasurable Anticipation

Sandplay therapists highly regard the initial and sometimes general countertransference experience of *pleasurable anticipation* as each client approaches the sand. The experience is described as "like looking at a dream." Words such as "mystery," "joy," "love," "fascination," "enthusiasm," "eagerness," and "reverence" are frequently mentioned, indicating an "umbrella" countertransference that may surround, hold, or even cover other less delightful aspects of the therapist's experience. One research participant explains the captivating ambiance of sandplay: "Sandplay entrances us, it enthralls us; it ignites the Self." There seems to be a trance-like quality, an altered state, an inescapable experience of surrender that permeates the work in the sand. As one participant explains: "It is the play zone; it's relaxing. I'm using a different part of my brain." In the words of yet another participant: "It is a place of such quietude. The outside world disappears, and there is a profound centering. It bypasses thinking; it is being and feeling." For one sandplay therapist, the pervasive experience itself is a poignant one: "a deeply felt, richly layered emotional experience that is also felt in the body, an experience of transcendent mutual humanness." Most of the participants mention that they are "fully present" to the sandplay process and they believe that this is of utmost importance for the client.

There is, indeed, at times, a sense of sandplay being "romanticized." However, within the prevalent experience of delight, most participants describe powerful countertransference experiences. I will discuss these experiences under the headings of Emotions; Experiential States; Intuitive States; Bodily Sensations; Thinking; Reverie, Fantasies, Memories, Dreams, and Images; and Numinous Experience.

Emotions

Sandplay therapists may experience the full range of human emotion as the process deepens — from joy, triumph, soothing, or comfort, to sadness, terror, horror and anger; from surprise or amazement to repulsion, irritation, or dread; from boredom to panic; and from utter desolation to uplifting hope and grace. Desire and expectation, confusion, and even erotic feelings are experienced as well. These feelings are qualitatively unique, depending upon the particular client, the sandworld, and the particular material being evoked in the unconscious. Surprisingly, experiences of "not feeling" or "feeling against" are also often mentioned.

Experiential States

Sandplay therapists reveal that their experiential states include intense concentration and focus, "primary maternal preoccupation," trance-like states, even feelings of resistance, interpersonal distancing, or feeling "pushed out." Particularly with repetitive or violent work in the sandtray, or with a stuck process or inauthentic-feeling sandtrays, the therapist is likely to experience confusion, boredom, doubt or self-questioning.

Intuitive States

Intuitive states — a sudden knowing without knowing why — are common in sandplay, sometimes experienced as a feeling of recognition, an "aha!," or an "Oh, yes!" Clarity is often mentioned as an important, even penetrating, experience for the therapist when a client makes a symbolic world in the sand. Yet several participants emphasize that this intuitive experience is often without thinking, without understanding, and without words.

Body Sensations

Body sensations arise for some therapists. While one participant states that she never has somatic countertransference, other participants mention at least one experience of being affected bodily or viscerally. Several times this is referred to as, "It got me in the gut." For two of the participants, somatic countertransference is an extremely important part of their experience of sandplay.

The strongest, most startling somatic reactions are associated with the terror that may accompany old trauma as it is evoked by work in the sand. Experiences such as "a quaking in my solar plexus," or "a clutching in my stomach," or "my body was tense, it was hard to breathe," or "it sent chills down my spine," are some of the most gripping experiences reported. Other somatic experiences are milder. These include sensations in the groin or in the heart, sensations of being sexually aroused, or of feeling as if one's own body is being massaged. Also reported are tingling or streaming sensations through the body, a relaxing or draining of tension from the body, and a sadness around the eyes. One participant describes the somatic experience of an electrical current running through her body during a numinous experience.

The breath is often mentioned, including descriptions such as a quick breath or a deep inhalation, a profound release, or an "Ahhhhh." A stopping of the breath, a sudden gasp, or a long deep exhalation are frequently reported. Interestingly, the breath seems to be connected not only with intense somatic experiences but also with the numinous experience. The breath is there when words are not.

Thinking

Several participants allude to "experiencing it in the gut, then conceptualizing it with thinking." Although many specifically mention that there is no thinking happening for them when a client is working in the sand, they report wondering, pondering, and a thoughtful questioning, or a curious interest, about the sandworld itself and about the relationship with the client. Several participants mention a "not knowing" or an "unknowing," or a "not understanding." While most seem to equate "holding" with tolerating their subjective experiences, several go further to mention struggling to put inchoate experiences into words, e.g., "digesting the information," or looking for the meaning in what they perceive to be a meaningful nonverbal communication within the transference/countertransference matrix.

Very often, accompanying a disturbing or confusing countertransference experience, there is also a worried, "Why can't I hold this well enough?" This seems to be due to the implicit influence of a kind of self blame related to personal or theoretical stances, such as the often stated, "How I hold it is the most important thing." There also seems to be the conviction that the therapist's full presence and good enough holding within the therapeutic relationship are the most important, fundamental aspects of the work. In keeping with these convictions is the belief that the therapist's failure to hold the process well enough or to connect deeply enough with the client might hamper the therapy.

The doubt and questioning involved in sandplay are quite striking. Along with "Why can't I hold it well enough?," sandplay therapists ask themselves questions like "What's happening here?," "What am I missing?," or even, "Does sandplay really work?" when the symbolic meaning of the process is not clear, when the images seem repetitive and without movement, or when the therapist feels she has in some way failed in her holding.

Reverie, Fantasies, Memories, Dreams, and Images

Some participants, in emphasizing the importance of their full presence in sandplay, deny that they experience reverie, although reverie does seem to occur in their descriptions of drifting into wondering, fantasies, memories, images, and dreams. However, these are less frequently mentioned than the experiences previously described.

Numinous Experience

Participants described the numinous experience in sandplay —which happens when the Self is "profoundly close" — as an experience beyond the personal. Although most of these therapists admit to being bewildered as to what a Self tray really is, they are clear about when they experience the numinous. It is like "entering a magical space," a timeless space that transcends words, where one is in a flow with the client, deeply connected and deeply affected by the awe, the reverence and the *Eros* experienced. Within this numinous field, there is a felt willingness to let the Other (both the other person and the unconscious) in. "The client enters a deep centering place, and there is a quiet joy in the connecting, and a sharing in the mystery of that." Within the numinosity, there is a knowing, a quieting, an experience of being profoundly stilled and awed, "like Holy Communion." It is a golden moment. It is an experience that is believed to transform both people in the therapeutic dyad.

For some of these therapists, the experience of awe seems to be limited to the numinous experience of the Self tray, but for others a kind of awe and reverence appear to be omnipresent in all of sandplay work. For one participant, the spiritual experience is the only identifiable experience within her total experience; for her, there is an "ever-present numinosity." For all the others, feeling, somatic, thinking and positive and negative imaginal experiences often enter the general experience of delight and pleasure.

To summarize, the subjective experience of the Jungian sandplay therapist encompasses a full range of ever-shifting emotions and experiential states, intuitions, bodily sensations, thinking, reverie, fantasies, memories, dreams, images, and numinosity. There is a general positive feeling — an "umbrella countertransference" — that often seems to hold the process. Within this common experience of delight and pleasure, however, exists a full and varied range of positive and negative feelings and experiences, and the pleasurable ambiance of sandplay can be ruptured by difficult and disturbing experiences for the therapist. Accompanying these experiences, there is often a sense of self doubt and self blame, perhaps because according to written theory and assumptions in sandplay they are not expected to occur. And yet, these are legitimate and valuable countertransference reactions, which may bring forth fuller experiences of the patient's trauma, helping to make it metabolizable in the therapist's body and psyche.

Examples of Negative Countertransference Experience in Sandplay

In addition to my findings (Cunningham, 2003), there are an increasing number of examples in the sandplay literature of negative countertransference experiences of intense affect, including horror, emptiness, dissociation, pain, suffering, and anxiety. They also include descriptions of projective identification found in complementary countertransference. Here are some early examples:

> Then I watched transfixed with awe and horror as he did a sand world of an innermost, fragile, undifferentiated, and deep part of himself, threatened by an enormous demonic figure. (Signell, 1981/1990a, p. 125)

> When I first saw this sand world it gave me a hard, empty feeling. (Signell, 1981/1990b, p. 170)

> At first this picture evokes immense pain, suffering and compassion. One feels it in both the heart and the stomach. (Ammann, 1991, p. 68)

> As we sat silently before his completed tray, I became aware of experiencing a tingling sensation, rising through my feet and into the rest of my body... I felt almost shaky, almost anxious myself. (Cunningham, 1997, p. 129)

I had a fantasy of her with a string of brightly colored images appearing above her head, each rapidly disappearing, replaced by yet another image from the dancing Fantasia of her psyche. My experience in my own body as I watched this colorful display was of dissociation: a fogginess, a spaciness, a sense of nothingness. (Cunningham, 1997, p. 131)

I was becoming aware of how exhausted and drained sessions with Gwen left me.... I found myself dreading her arrival. (Margoliash, 1998, p. 74)

As she worked I was filled with grief. (Chiaia, 1998, p. 99)

I had a painful feeling that I had never felt before. In my body I saw and felt pain and death. I searched for hope but it was not found. (Montecchi, 1999, pp. 26-27)

While Anna made her sand picture, I felt a sense of malaise, almost corresponding to the stomach ache she described when she talked about the abuser. This malaise was very complex. I felt a sense of emptiness and abdominal pain, a feeling of discontinuity in my body's own surface, a loss of spatial references to the point of not knowing where I was sitting or where the chair was with respect to the table. [In the next session] these feelings centered on a sort of disorganization of movement and thought. My ability to think was paralyzed. (Montecchi, 1999, p. 40)

I felt petrified, immobile, bodiless, heartless, rigid and passive, just like Emmanuel. (Rocco, 2000, p. 59)

I was beginning to feel anxious, frustrated, incompetent as I imagined her mother must have felt. (Winter, 2000, p. 42)

I had a feeling of vagueness and an image of fog. (Chiaia, 2001, p. 21)

The analyst felt a sudden discomfort, nearly nausea.... It was accompanied by a strong feeling that 'everything is hostile.' He also noted that objects or forms with which he was well acquainted — like the pattern of the carpet in his office — had changed. Festoons of flowers which had always looked like festoons of flowers now suddenly looked like evil claws; even the carpet's usually pleasant colors screamed out and attacked each other. The office became an entirely intolerable world. As he grasped the feeling that 'everything is hostile, the world is evil,' his nausea had somewhat subsided. (Pattis, 2002, p. 34-35)

In addition to these examples, Jackson (1991) and Berman (1993) describe obvious negative countertransference responses to sandtrays in both consultation and research groups. Jackson asked her consultation group to focus on the feeling response evoked by each sandtray. Intellectual curiosity makes it difficult for group members to stay with these reactions, which are in fact obvious from the members' body language, including "painful winces, shudders, sharp inhaling gasps, tensing shoulders and bodies pulling back" (p. 57). Berman (1993) reports that when shown slides of incest survivors' sandtrays, her research participants show a qualitative change, such as sighing, nervous laughter, rustling of papers, getting up to stretch — all unconscious nonverbal reactions. Her participants are unable to stay with and contain their experience. These examples point to the importance of recognizing and containing negative countertransference responses. Rather than leaving them unrecognized, and perhaps avoided or acted out, it is crucial to become mindfully aware of them, to find the meaning in them and to use it for healing.

Chapter 8

Co-Transference: Moving Toward A Relational Theory

And so it is with the intangible thread of the human spirit. It cannot be seen; it can only be felt.

— *Harold Stone, 1980, p. 16*

A relational approach views the therapist and her subjective experience as an inherent part of the therapy. Transference and countertransference are, in this view, *co-created* in a mutual, reciprocal process, revealing important, repeated themes in the dance toward wholeness. These themes manifest in the *total situation,* and are sometimes made known as a *background feel* to the session.

In this dance, difficult countertransference experiences arise and we may need help in digesting them. For example, if a sandplay scene makes us feel anxious, *there is meaning in the anxiety.* It is something to be investigated and understood through consultation, therapy, and our own soul searching. As stated by Jung (1946/1966), our feelings *will* get in the way in our entanglement with the client's feelings and this "chemical combination" (p. 3) will lead to a transformation of both. The rainmaker metaphor indicates that we need to put ourselves right — sometimes through therapy or consultation — and that this *coming to understanding* within the therapist is actually healing for the client, *whether or not it is spoken aloud* (Schore, 2003). The sandplay therapist's attunement to her own subjective experience may deepen her awareness of the *meaning* embedded in the relational field.

Kay Bradway's "Co-Transference"

The therapeutic relationship is a mix, a complex mix, a valuable mix. It is this mix that I am referring to when I use the term co-transference.

— *Bradway & McCoard, 1997*

Kay Bradway moves sandplay toward a relational sensibility and reconciles some of the aforementioned discrepancies between theory and experience with her concept of "co-transference," which is clearly a field view of transference/countertransference. Within the concept of co-transference she has made room for the possibility of negative experience. Until Bradway's (1991; Bradway & McCoard, 1997) work on co-transference, most writers on the subject of sandplay appear to accept without question the implicit notion of positive transference/countertransference.[24]

While Bradway's definition of the co-transference is very close to the contemporary definition of transference/countertransference as the total subjective experience of therapist with client and client with therapist, there are a few significant theoretical points I'd like to explore.

There is usually a positive affective tone connected with the use of the word co-transference. It is often used to indicate *countertransference of a positive nature*. The term co-transference is also sometimes used to indicate the transference/countertransference mix, regardless of the positive or negative feel. However, some sandplay therapists continue to use the word countertransference only if they are referring to a negative experience. From Bradway's writings, we know that co-transference is the

---

[24] Again, I am not questioning the necessity for the therapist to provide both freedom and protection. I am questioning the implication that he/she will have only positive, protective feelings within the free and protected space.

therapeutic feeling relationship between therapist and client, containing experiential states and feelings that go back and forth simultaneously on conscious and unconscious levels. She states that positive transference is necessary for any therapy to take place — and, again, current findings from neuroscience agree. She also describes some rather unconscious — though mild — negative feelings, as witnessed in the behavior of client and therapist or revealed in the sandtray.

Bradway is clearly describing a *concordant countertransference,* where, in her words, the therapist is *feeling with* the self of the client. "Co-transference" seems to exclude Racker's (1957/1972) view of *complementary countertransference* because it would be experienced as a *feeling against;* however, we may also understand it as a *feeling with* the client's *internal objects.* The theoretical stance of needing to be exclusively "feeling with" the client might deny us full access to our countertransference experience. Particularly in trauma work, the therapist may feel taken over by feelings of distress, and this is so disturbing that it could, if not properly understood, be considered a "feeling against," and because this is understood as threatening to the free and protected space, it might then be dissociated or repressed by the therapist.

However, Bradway (Bradway & McCoard, 1997) makes it clear that love and hate are both acceptable and necessary feelings in the co-transference, and states that "the co-transference is always there" (p. 47). Yet, she also implies that co-transference has a particular quality of trust and is not as random in holding the infinite possibilities of positive and negative feelings and complexes as one would expect in the entire range of transference/countertransference.

Bradway's point regarding the necessity of safety, trust, and positive transference in sandplay is well taken. Yet, questions arise. How are we to understand co-transference in relation to the "feeling against" that arises with a client's preverbal or nonverbal trauma? Is co-transference actually the same as transference/countertransference? Is there a place in co-transference for the more intense affects, such as rage, terror, anxiety, or shame? What about confusion, deadness, or even more disturbing experiences of fragmentation or annihilation? Or is co-transference limited to *a special quality of field* in the transference/countertransference?

Bradway (Bradway and McCoard, 1997) connects co-transference with Winnicott's (1971) transitional space and also with Goodheart's (1980) *secured-symbolizing space*[25] and makes these the theoretical ground of sandplay. She states, "This third area, this area of illusion or area of experience, is exactly the place where the sandplay process occurs" (Bradway & McCoard, 1997, p. 9). And yet, there are times, as Winnicott (1971) pointed out, when we need to bring the client into transitional space, into a state of being able to play. He wrote:

> Psychotherapy takes place in the overlap of two areas
> of playing, that of the patient and that of the therapist.
> Psychotherapy has to do with two people playing together.
> The corollary of this is that where playing is not possible the
> work done by the therapist is directed towards bringing the
> patient from a state of not being able to play into a state of
> being able to play.... (p. 38)

Yet, how might we do this? A close reading of Goodheart (1980; also see Chapter 2 of this writing) reveals that he discussed not only the *secured-symbolizing* field, but two other *pre-symbolic* fields as well — fields where "playing" cannot yet occur, fields that are more difficult, painful, or disturbing for the therapist, and in which a complementary countertransference may be more likely to occur. The *secured-symbolizing* quality of co-transference leaves out the deadening, trying, often sensory-laden counter-transference experience of Goodheart's (1980) *persona-restoring field,* and the disturbing, painful, emotionally intense experiences in the *complex-discharging field.*

Although it is richly rewarding to work in the *secured-symbolizing* field, it is helpful to hold our work within a broader context of other possible fields. Remember that Goodheart states that no symbolic work such as sandplay can happen in a field other than the secured-symbolizing

---

[25] I am indebted to Brian Lukas for first pointing this out to me.

field. I strongly disagree. However, the work is somewhat different in a non-symbolizing field. If we bring the work of Bion to inform our own work in more difficult relational fields — slow symbolic work that includes containing internal states and making meaning of unconscious communications — sandplay is not only possible but transformative.

Quite often, we have no choice but to work in *pre-symbolic fields.* And although the *secured-symbolizing* field has traditionally been favored by Jungians and sandplay therapists, the cross-fertilization of information from psychoanalysis expands Jungian practice into these earlier two fields as well. Any of these fields may arise at any time; however, with some clients, a particular field may be pervasive in the therapy.

Equating transitional space and the *secured-symbolizing* field with "exactly the place where the sandplay process occurs" (Bradway & McCoard, 1997, p. 9) may be limiting. Getting to transitional space is often understood as a developmental achievement; many of our clients are simply not there yet — they cannot yet think symbolically or truly play. It is our job to help them get there. To limit sandplay to transitional space eliminates many clients who could benefit from sandplay, but not in the same way as clients who are already able to enter into symbolic realms.

So, we are left with a sense of co-transference as tied to the more colorful *secured-symbolizing* field and transitional space. *Clearly, this describes the predominant countertransference experience in sandplay.* Yet, from the examples of disturbing or disorienting countertransference now arising in the literature, it is not the only possible experience.

Bradway makes a valuable beginning, laying the groundwork for further important theoretical discussion. It is likely that the meaning of co-transference will continue to evolve.

In Part III, I will use the work of Goodheart and Ogden to shed light on earlier, presymbolic fields that are qualitatively different from — and more countertransferentially difficult than — the *secured-symbolizing* field.

The Wounded Healer Archetype

In accord with Racker, Jung repeatedly reminds us that we are all wounded healers (Sedgwick, 1994). In our negative complementary countertransference experiences, our own woundedness becomes activated and we may react by automatically defending against it. Reowning our own part in this is one of the most difficult things we are called upon to do as therapists. Yet, Jung makes clear that in our own wounded places we apprehend the wounded places of the other. Using mindfulness, we can allow ourselves to be affected by these unbearable experiences, to surrender to them, be changed by them, and work to put ourselves right in the world of the countertransference. Through inner work on ourselves, an internal coming into the natural flow of things happens.

Chapter 9

Resonance:
The Sandplay Therapist's Subjective Experience of the Co-created Relational Field

Relationship is a pattern of energy exchange over time.

— *Daniel Siegel, 2004*

A Feeling Connection

The importance of establishing a "feeling connection" between client and therapist is emphasized in sandplay theory. In sandplay, the feeling connection accessed through the bridge of countertransference is frequently called "resonance," a term that beautifully captures the combination of empathic immersion and attunement to self required of the sandplay therapist (Ammann, 1991, Amatruda & Helm Simpson, 1997). Amman (1994) explains resonance thus:

> The principle of resonance is very simple. If you have in your hands a violin with four strings and another violin with four strings lying on the table beside you, the strings on the violin on the table will start to vibrate as soon as you start to play your violin.

> If you ... have an instrument with only two strings, only two strings of the violin on the table will start to move. If you have a miraculous violin with ten strings, then not only will the violin on the table pick up all the vibrations, but perhaps a lute hanging on the wall or a magic harp somewhere in the room will also begin to quiver. (p. 58)

Ammann (1991) also gives us one of the most full and beautiful descriptions of the countertransference experience found in sandplay literature:

> ... what become active in me are the more instinctual, physical reactions. These depend on subtle sensory perceptions, body feelings, and intuition and on an empathic, emotional relationship with the analysand. This does not happen unconsciously but rather from a conscious turning toward the more receptive attitude which can grip the whole person. (p. 6)

This emphasizes the therapist's task of being consciously receptive to unconscious communications from the client, with an emphasis on *knowing with the body.* Our own subjective experience, or resonance, is the container for these mysterious energies of the relational field. Transference/countertransference is an ongoing, resonating, embedded melody that permeates the relational container in any therapy, including sandplay work. The quality of the relationship and the energies moving back and forth between therapist and patient are an implicit part of each sandworld, inseparable from it — not something from the outside that occasionally impacts the sandplay.

Resonance is an inherent quality of the relational field. Psychic energies of client and therapist co-mingle, and the ambiance that contains and informs subtly changes as the relationship deepens. Sandplay takes place from within a therapeutic relationship, and is a vehicle through which feelings and experiences in the transference/countertransference field may show up visually *and* be felt experientially. The symbolic understanding of sandplay needs to be grounded in the reality of the flow of psychic energies in the clinical relationship.

Resonance and Projective Identification:
Experiencing Through the Other
or *Understanding from the Inside Out*

We may think of projective identification as an aspect of resonance. The concept of projective identification, what Sands (1997a) calls *experiencing through the other* has made possible the paradigm shift from an intrapsychic stance to a more relational psychoanalysis (Aron, 1996). There may be times in which the client seems to be communicating dissociated or preverbal aspects of self-experience in a gripping way through the therapist's experience, rather than — or along with — through the image in the sandtray. Through discoveries in neuroscience, such as the reality of right brain-to-right brain communication, clinicians have become aware of the variety of ways that trauma, locked in implicit realms, may reveal itself either during verbal therapy or a sandplay process, thus making it more available for healing.

Projective identification has been considered as merely a pathological process by some, probably because it was initially understood in a pathologizing way. But the concept has evolved (Bion, 1967/1988) to include a hope in the other, as well as a path for communication and psychological change (Ogden, 1982). This mode of communication is used by all of us sometimes, but more pervasively in infants and in some clients, particularly those with early attachment trauma. One might say that it is a very human experience to sometimes communicate this way.

Receiving and understanding projective identification enables the therapist to experience a profound empathy. Pointing out the importance of receptivity to information provided by projective identification, Sands (1997a) says that certain clients may have a need

> ...to communicate certain unsymbolized, affective experience through the other's experience in order to explore vicariously and integrate intolerable aspects of self. It is a need to feel understood by the other *from the inside out*. (p. 664)

However, it can be an arduous process for the therapist to get to empathy because the client is unconsciously communicating to the therapist a disturbing, unverbalized experience that the client has not been able to integrate. Many sandplay therapists report that the client's unsymbolized experience may manifest itself not only in the sandtray, but also in the body of the therapist viscerally. Here's an example from a research interview:

> As she works in the sand, a client who has experienced early sexual and relational trauma with her mother, mentions that she has thoughts of death. *I experience heaviness, sleepiness.* She places two black pots in the sand, and then a canoe and a baby. She rolls a black pot around in the sand. *I experience a trance-like feeling.* She moves a pot through the sand. *I feel panic.* She says, "I just went away, I didn't want to be here." *I wonder: is my experience of panic related to her dissociation?* She buries the whole pot with the baby in it. She takes the baby out and buries it separately, then takes it out and moves it around the tray. *I notice that this is very serious play.* She tries to put the baby in the pot. *Again, I feel a flash of panic.* She puts the baby on top of the pot and says that this is less scary. *I feel relieved.* She puts the baby in the boat and moves it around. *I feel panic.* Then she brings in an angel. She lodges the baby on the angel's wing and moves them around together. The baby is almost bigger than the angel, but fits perfectly, cuddled into her wings. *I wonder if she thinks I'm big enough to hold her.* She says she wants to shut her eyes. *I notice that I feel sleepy too.*

Projective identification may be experienced in the countertransference as an experiential state or image, such as "fogginess" (Cunningham, 1997, p. 131), "an image of fog" (Chiaia, 2001, p. 21), or "an oriental carpet" (Cunningham, 1999). These experiences or images may present as background phenomena to the session, not yet quite consciously experienced by the therapist.

Another way to think about projective identification is hinted at by Beebe (as cited in Bradway & McCoard, 1997, p. xi-xii). He says that the image in the sand expresses a feeling state and represents accretions of the Self. These accretions, or integrates and deintegrates of the Self, are activated through projective identification processes (Schwartz-Salant, 1988;

Gordon, 1965). Projective identification is an aspect of resonance in which the Self moves toward wholeness.

We feel the complexity of trying to hold both the visual, sensate sandplay experience with the visceral and emotional experiences that may occur in the therapist. Add to this the necessity to attend to our own experience of the symbol as well as its archetypal meanings. Resonance — which may include visceral experiences, emotions, mental images, or background states — may in fact *predict* or *verify* the therapist's understanding of the image in the sand. Again, I quote Samuels (1989):

> If countertransference communications are both images and bodily visions then body and image shimmer together almost to the point of fusion. (p. 165)

I believe that the shimmering together of body and image is involved in the synchronistic moment as we silently begin to understand our experience of resonance. In sandplay, the client's inner world may become symbolized silently in the self of the therapist, as well as in the sandworld. Indeed, projective identification and countertransference may hold images that actually foretell the symbol.

Weinrib (1983) describes the Jungian view of the symbol as "a healing agent that acts as a reconciling bridge between the opposites" (p. 23). This is an apt description of countertransference, as well.[26] Countertransference, or resonance, is the symbol coming alive in the therapist's body.

---

[26] It is interesting to note the bridging capacities of the symbol, the transcendent function, projective identification, and countertransference.

Summary of Parts I and II

The use of countertransference — a central technique in contemporary psychoanalytically informed psychotherapy — is a deep, meditative investigation of the therapist's unconscious experience in relation to the Other. The concept of countertransference has evolved from its early construction as interference with therapeutic work to the current realization that the therapist's subjective experiences in relation to the client hold important unconscious communications from the client and the field. The therapist needs to be exquisitely attuned to these communications. Her emotional, bodily, thinking and imaginal responses to her client are a vast source of information about the client's unconscious (as well as about the therapist's vulnerabilities) and can lead to a fuller understanding of what needs to be healed in the between and surround.

Countertransference is the other source of the symbol. Any countertransference experience — positive or negative — may be a healing bridge to the Other. It often facilitates the transcendent function, uniting the opposites of conscious and unconscious.

Our metaphors for healing are tremendously important in helping us through rough spots in a therapy. In sandplay, positive countertransference has been revered and embraced. At the same time, confusing, disturbing, or stuck places in countertransference are not *explicitly* considered to be *useful* in healing. Yet, remedying this absence of countertransference theory in sandplay could provide a map to the unknown or confusing territories on the journey of healing. Without such a map, the sandplay therapist is left in shame and self-doubt when she is confronted with an intensity of subjective experience not usually attributed to Kalff's (1980) "free and protected space."

Dissociated, stuck, or intensely disturbing experiences are indeed a part of the subjective experience of the sandplay therapist, but sandplay therapists need guidelines for normalizing or using them. These kinds of experiences have rarely, until recently, been mentioned in the sandplay literature, and this holds important implications for sandplay theory: it is evolving. Sandplay therapists have been struggling to articulate a more relational view. Toward this end, I will present in Part III a theory of relational fields that addresses a full range of the subjective experience of the therapist within the relational container provided.

Note: the following theory is not at all intended to be used for pathologizing self or others. Please use it as a description of completely normal human experiences.

Part III

Relational Sandplay Theory

Yet sand itself is not related. For this, people are needed.
And the people must have heart, and must have been
through their journey, just as the sand has.

The people to hold the liminal space must be a little eroded,
and they must have been through the fire, and fallen
from the mountain tops, and blown through the air,
and tossed and been lost in the sea.
[After this initiation] ... the psyche can only be approached
with humility and awe.

— *Kate Amatruda, 1997*

In relational sandplay theory, our relational experiences are named and normalized, and may therefore be easier to live through and understand. Our experiences of blankness, emptiness, confusion, turmoil — even gut-wrenching, traumatic experience — as well as the flow of symbolic meaning in transitional or numinous space, become recognizable and explainable. An integrated understanding of experiential states, affects, and images allows our felt experience to inform our holding of the visual symbol. We can then more effectively use our resonance to embody the image held in the sandtray and the ambiance of shifting relational fields.

Chapter 10

The Four Archetypal Relational Fields in Sandplay

The birth of a heart-connection is really the key to field experiences.

— Nathan Schwartz-Salant, 1995

Field theories explicating relational experience have created a sea change in many approaches to psychotherapy, a sea change that is beginning to reach sandplay therapy as well (Bradway & McCoard; 1997, Lukas, 2001; and Chiaia, 2003).

In this chapter, I introduce a relational fields theory for sandplay,[27] identifying and describing four archetypal[28] modes of relational experience. These relational fields arise between therapist and client, surrounding and holding them as they move through experiences of aliveness and deadness, love and strife, the numinous and the mundane. These fields describe the

---

[27] Much of this chapter, in slightly different form, first appeared in the *Journal of Sandplay Therapy,* 2004, (2).

[28] In this chapter, I draw mainly from the work of Goodheart (1980) and Ogden (1989, 1994). We may suspect that these three or four fields of human experiencing are fundamental aspects of human experience, as other theorists have discovered and elaborated similar fields (Mitchell, 2000; Spiegelman & Mansfield, 1996; Schwartz-Salant, 1995; Langs, 1978a, 1978b, 1979; Langs and Searles, 1980; and Searles, 1965).

nature of the engagement with the Other and how it may be experienced, understood, and therapeutically used. Uncovering the symbolic meaning of relational fields can illuminate sandplay processes that may otherwise be troubling or difficult to understand.

The more demanding clinical experiences that bewilder and stymie the clinician almost always involve a difficult countertransference experience. In sandplay, such experiences often arise when sandtrays don't make sense from a traditional sandplay understanding. We see sandtrays that are apparently without symbolic movement, and those that are barren, chaotic, or deeply disturbing. We also encounter so-called "pretty trays" and other sandtrays that seem symbolically uninterpretable. Sandtrays of this nature may be intertwined with upsetting or confusing countertransferences of sleepiness, boredom, agitation, anxiety or despair. Perhaps because of this, these sandtrays are sometimes thought to indicate that the sandplay process is not viable or that the therapist is not "holding" the process well enough. Either of these could be true, but I would like to propose a third possibility: that these uncomfortable experiences can be understood as signs of emerging relational fields, each with profoundly informative relational qualities that manifest both in the tray and in the subjective experience of the therapist.

Relational sandplay theory recognizes four qualities of human experience — relational fields — that also exist within the therapeutic relationship:

Field One: *The Field of Original Oneness/Merger*

Field Two: *The Field of Twoness/Rupture*

Field Three: *The Field of Differentiated Oneness/Transitional Space*

Field Four: *The Numinous Field*

The first two of the fields, *The Field of Original Oneness/Merger* and *The Field of Twoness/Rupture,* have never before been described in the sandplay literature. Both arise from the client's *relational trauma,* which reverberates in the field between therapist and client. *Each particular field arises because that is where the healing needs to happen.* Recognizing these fields offers a framework for working with confusing or disturbing countertransference experience, and helps the therapist more closely attune to her client.

Field Three, *The Field of Differentiated Oneness/Transitional Space,* is characterized by fluid empathic connection and the meaningful use of the symbol. This field is well-understood and has been thoroughly explored in the sandplay literature. In fact, this is the field in which the vast majority of published sandplay cases occur.

Field Four, *The Numinous Field* arises from Field Three (O'Connell, 1986) and is the ever present, sacred container, the holding provided by the therapist and his/her own connection with the Self. It may also arise as the felt sense of awe that accompanies the constellation of the Self so familiar to Jungian sandplay therapists. Field Four is a shared, transcendent, relational experience of the union of conscious and unconscious, and it is an experience completely void of anxiety.

I will examine the four fields, working from the most primitively based to the most developed. It is important, however, to keep in mind that while based on human development, these fields are also archetypally present as fundamental aspects of human experience throughout life. They are snapshots of a flow of ever-shifting experiential states. *In psychological health, all four fields are muted states and oscillate easily.* Each may be thought of as a different way of both experiencing anxiety and attributing meaning to experience (Ogden, 1994).

With some clients, the therapeutic dyad may find itself almost exclusively within a single field for some time, or even for most of the therapy. Other dyads may cycle in and out of different fields even within a given therapeutic hour. These fields are fluid and, in practice, rarely exist in pure form. With the use of the sandtray, a noticeable shift to a field different from the field that is constellated in the verbal therapy may occur.

Each field has a different "feel" to the therapist. In Field One, the countertransference experience is often a sensory, pre-symbolic one where symbolic meaning is difficult or impossible to find. Boredom, confusion and emptiness are the predominant feeling states. In contrast, when we find ourselves in Field Two, our subjective experience is one of intense affective turmoil and discontinuity. In this field we feel held captive in relational conflict. In Field Three we find fluent empathy, a felt sense of connectedness and meaningful use of the symbol. Sometimes, Field Three leads us into Field Four (O'Connell, 1986). Here, we experience the numinosity of the Self.

Let us look more closely at each field.

Field One: The Field of Original Oneness/Merger

Field One, the Field of Original Oneness/Merger, is a field of relational trauma and *pre-symbolized* experiencing. In it, the therapist often feels merged, yet simultaneously out of contact, with the client. This may feel distant or that no connection exists at all. In this field, the client needs to use others as containers for unbearable, unnameable experience (Bion, 1963/1977). From a Self Psychology perspective, this field conveys the urgent necessity to feel cohesive and whole through the use of selfobjects (Kohut, 1971). Developmentally, this attempt at oneness may mean that trauma has too early interrupted mother-infant oneness. Because of this very early injury to the self, this field may often have a stuck quality, with little feeling of symbolic movement and no sign of transcendent functioning.

Countertransference experience in the field of Original Oneness/ Merger has come to my attention through my research, work with some of my own clients, cases presented by my colleagues, and several articles (Cunningham, 1997, 1999; Montecchi, 1999; Rocco, 2000; Chiaia, 2001). Pre-symbolized experiencing means that the therapist's experience in this field tends to be *sensory rather than emotional or thinking*. The sensations may include dizziness or confusion, a watery feeling, a feeling of dissolving into space, or even a sense of deadness. We may feel disconnected or unable to think; objects or people in space may feel distorted. Or we may feel controlled, empty, or paralyzed. In any of these Field One experiences, the therapist will feel held at bay, ineffective, or completely useless. The most easily recognizable hallmarks of the field of Original Oneness/Merger are boredom, sleepiness, anxiety, or dissociation.

Although superficially it may seem like communication is taking place in this field of Original Oneness/Merger, the words or images provided by the client often do not transmit meaning (Goodheart, 1980). Rather, they are used as a *shield* for protection from the other. This indicates an unconscious desperate need for protection and safety. For the client, the essence of this field is defense against retraumatization in relationship.

With deeper attunement to our own countertransference experience of this field, we may feel both longing and a sense of deadness. The client in the field of Original Oneness/Merger is silently communicating something like: "I am despairing (or lonely or anxious). I want you near me to understand my experience. But don't come too close, because I am terrified that you will hurt me as others have." Attempting to merge in this distancing way provides contact with — yet safe distance and protection from — the desired other. The therapist's task is to "decode the sounds of distress" embedded in the field (McDougall, 1993, p. 299).

A sandplay therapist gives an example of her countertransference in Field One:

> As I sit with a seven-year-old boy on his birthday, I experience the following: He says something that sounds like nonsense; I don't get it. As he works in the dry sandtray, I think his sessions are dry. The game of Risk he frequently plays is uninspired. His play is not aggressive. I notice there is a reasonable amount of movement in the sandtray. Things are in and out — mines — or minds? I go in and out in my attention. He tells his story in a monotone. It is involved but not related. I try to question him, but there is not much there. He is involved but not related. There are confusing changes in his story. *I wonder if this is related to his early trauma with switching mothers.* He touches me ever so slightly as he speaks about aliens coming down. He wants to know about my other clients, wants to know their names. He is interested in me. He becomes confused about time. I remind him that next week he won't be here. He doesn't want to leave; he hangs on. I spend a long time cleaning up after him. Some objects are buried, like the baby that he said was dying... (as cited in Cunningham, 2003, p. 176)

In this session my colleague's experience is typical of Field One: dissociation, boredom, confusion. Also, typically, she notices her attention coming and going. Her mind is in and out, intermittently wandering off into reverie or blankness and then back into the session. As in this example, there is often a feeling of dryness, barrenness or emptiness in the field and/or in the sandtray. In pre-symbolic interaction, we often apprehend *a sensory experience* rather than affect, or narrative, or symbolic meaning. Because of this, the entire interaction, including the sandtray, may be better understood from the therapist's countertransference experience of the field rather than from the symbolic content in the tray.

In the session, because of early relational trauma, this client desperately tries to connect, but at the same time tries to keep the Other —the unconscious and the therapist — at a safe distance. There is unconscious terror at the possibility of connection, brought home by the therapist's reverie about "switching mothers." Yet his desire to connect is poignantly expressed in his curiosity about the therapist and her clients and in attempting to linger after the session is over.

Sandtrays in this field may be stark and barren, with few figures, or without any figures at all. The trays may be chaotic, superficial, or seemingly lacking in symbolic meaning. Other times, although quite visually beautiful, the trays may feel inauthentic — so-called "pretty trays." With these trays, the lack of symbolic meaning is to be found in the therapist's subjective experience of profound dissociation and deadness or blankness, as she resonates with an unconscious feeling state inside the client. When one enters the field of Original Oneness/Merger, where words and images have no symbolic meaning, one must often fall back on the countertransference to decode the conveyed pre-symbolic meaning. Countertransference is the bridge between the unconscious and consciousness as well as the *other* source of the symbol.

Ogden (1989) points to an element of this field when he describes the *autistic-contiguous* position, a mode of experience in which raw sensory data are organized through forming pre-symbolic connections between sensory experiences and bounded surfaces. This represents the client's effort to keep the self from leaking away when an early containing Other has not been adequately available. Clinically we may see many symptoms of this, such as humming, hair twirling, nonstop talking, continual stroking of the face, extensively layered clothing, all of which may be understood as efforts to find one's edges, to contain and soothe the self. With adequate containment from the Other, these experiences of soft and hard edges become the ground for the creation of symbols. Ogden writes, "It is on these surfaces that the experience of the self has its origins" (p. 49). Use of the sandtray provides a felt experience of edges and shapes. Sometimes, trays in this field do not hold figures, but consist only of working in the sand. Often in this field, words (and perhaps sandplay) are used as a protective barrier, like a second skin (Bick, 1968.)

In this field, language may become an *act* rather than a means to communicate. This distinction may be disturbing or confusing for the therapist. Yet, this way of communicating has a purpose for the client: speech or sandplay become an attempt *to make the therapist experience something*. This form of communication results from early traumas that diminish the client's capacity to think about himself and to contain painful emotions.

McDougall (1993) explains the fundamental need to be connected, and the purpose this form of *non*-communication might serve:

> *Communication*—from the Latin communicare: to render common, to be in relationship with, to be connected—reveals its underlying etymological and affective meaning. All people in certain situations, and some people much of the time, use verbal communication literally as a way of maintaining a contact, being in relation with, or even being part of, "common to," another person.
>
> This vital link to the Other may override in importance the symbolic function which consists of the desire to inform someone of something, and can take the form of crying, calling out, screaming, growling rather than *telling* something. (p. 287)

Non-symbolic communication is both a way of remaining in intimate connection and also of conveying and discharging emotion directly.

The intent is to cause the Other to share a pain that cannot yet be expressed through language or through the meaningful use of symbols in the tray. The therapist is likely to feel bewildered and invaded by such experiences unless she looks closely for the meaning in them. According to McDougall, this "fusional communication" is "a demand to be heard rather than listened to, a need for communion rather than communication" (p. 289). It conveys unnameable dread. This is pre-symbolic suffering that has no words or conscious images, a state that makes it unsafe to trust another with one's own vulnerability.

Another example (from my own practice) illustrates experience in the field of Original Oneness/Merger:

Figure 1: The Blue Heart. "I sensed not only her fear underlying her need to push me away with words, but also her longing to feel loved, to have a heart connection." Field One of Original Oneness/Merger.

The Blue Heart

As I sit with a 34-year-old client, I am impressed with how much she sounds like a teenager. She uses adolescent language and complains nonstop about her friends mistreating her.

Her tone is aggressive, yet I know she is hurting. She seems so alone in her hostile world. Even though her conversation is animated and lively, I can find no meaning in the barrage of words coming at me. My mind feels paralyzed, and sometimes I am overcome by drowsiness. I search my experience for something to say to her — anything — and yet on those rare occasions when words come to me, there is no space for them. I mirror her the best I can, with my facial expressions and soothing sounds. I know that she feels very attached to me, yet I experience myself as useless and dull.

One day she decides to make a sandtray but can think of nothing to do with the sand. I encourage her to simply get her hands into it. She lightly brushes its surface for a long time and then eventually digs deeper to make the shape of a blue heart at the bottom of the tray *(Figure 1)*. I experience a "Yes!" inside myself. Chattering all the while, she barely seems to notice what she has made. Then she stops and says, "Oh, do you think that's what is missing?" She places her hands on either side of the heart, pressing her handprints into the sand. She then feels embarrassed and dismisses her tray as a "lack of creativity" and does not touch the sand again for many years.

For me, this is a poignant moment. Yes, I think, the feelings are missing. Yet the blue heart guarded by handprints seems to leave its mark. I sense not only her fear underlying the need to push me away with words, but also her longing to feel loved, to have a heart connection. I suspect that we might circle around this desire in our relationship for a long time before getting to her feelings: the real heart of the matter. We need to slowly release the sadness she didn't know she felt, and the shame at leaving her own unique emotional mark in the world. She needs to grieve, and to gradually become more conscious of her own sadness and longing to be loved.

Hidden beneath this experience of deadness, aliveness is buried in the unconscious longing. In this field it is in moments like these that, if we as therapists are able to look deeply enough into our own experience, we will

107

feel the client's painful longing for connection, inherently protected and camouflaged.

During a pervasive experience of Field One, sandplay work itself may reveal the dissociated meaning and emotions. When this does not happen, we may feel an urgency to vacate this field by problem solving, making referrals, or recommending medication. But the real work of this field is actually *in* the deadness or emptiness. The barrenness, disappointment, futility, and dissociation need to be recognized and contained by the therapist and worked with internally — perhaps through a countertransference image — until an in-between space begins to form, a space where the symbol can come out and play.

Without a deep understanding of this field, work in it may be devalued as being infertile or outside the space of creative transformation. Goodheart's (1980) observations of his *persona-restoring* field apply to the field of Original Oneness/Merger, but only up to a point. While I agree with Goodheart that this field may feel like an "out of contact" field, I do not agree that sandplay in this field "serves a mutual deception" (p. 5). When we expect that sandplay will take place only in a fully symbolizing field, we miss the important authentic unsymbolized experience that is all the while being communicated. The therapist who understands this may be better able to work with patients in this field, whether through the use of verbal therapy or sandplay. The *total situation* must be apprehended in the effort to understand sandplay in the field of Original Oneness.

Attunement to the Other through our own self experience becomes vitally important in Field One. McDougall (1993) tells us that "... an attitude of expectant silence" (appropriate in Field Three) means desolation and death to these patients ... they need to exist in other people's eyes, to feel truly alive" (p. 301). So, the appropriate intervention here is not silence nor interpretation, but active mirroring, and a conscious creating of potentially vital *space* for the feelings and thoughts to come into being. Ogden (1989) confirms that pathology in this field is characterized by a lack of internal "potential" space. He writes:

To the extent that the bodily system is closed off from mutually transforming experiences with human beings, there is an absence of "potential space" (Winnicott, 1971, Ogden, 1985b, 1986) between oneself and the other (a potential psychological space between self-experience and sensory perception). This closed bodily world is a world without room in which to create a distinction between symbol and symbolized, and therefore a world in which there is no possibility for the coming into being of an interpreting subject; it is a world in which there is no psychological space between the infant and the mother in which transitional phenomena might be created/discovered. (p. 60)

To understand this more deeply, we must look at the concepts of transitional phenomena and symbolization. What follows is a Jungian and psychoanalytic integration, closely following Donelan's (1999) excellent description of this process, bringing together Winnicott, Neumann, and Fordham's points of view. When the Self's archetypal expectations have been reliably met by the environment mother in a good enough way over time, the Self integrates a reliable image of this mother. This happens through the mother holding the infant's experience over time, existing as undifferentiated mother-infant, and living an experience together that allows for going-on being.

The infant must have a good, solid experience of undifferentiated oneness and a secure internal image of mother before he can tolerate separateness. Transitional space, or "space between," does not occur until the infant is threatened with the mother's absence. Separateness is achieved and made tolerable first through a good enough mothering experience and then through the use of a transitional object, such as a special blanket or soft toy. A transitional object, by definition, is never given; it is both created and discovered by the infant. It is the infant's ability to use something in play space and transform it into *something else* that makes possible relinquishing of the mother as a real person in order to experience her as a symbol. Campbell (2004) writes,

For the creation of transitional objects, there must be available some "transitional space," in which the child can imaginatively elaborate the object. In this space some degree of "illusion" springs up, which allows us to have faith that reality will match, at least sufficiently, what we need. (p. 1)

When this developmental process does not go well — due to excessive, unrelieved anxiety, hunger or distress — there is a collapse of going-on-being causing premature ego development. This interrupts the process of assimilating an internal image of the mother because the infant takes on this role himself. Such a self-sufficient maneuver leaves the infant without an internalized image of mother to use for a feeling of security when the mother is not there. Therefore, the symbolic attitude is arrested in the child. Without this symbolic attitude, the ego defends against the unconscious and is unable to make use of the transcendent function. In therapy, the therapist holds the transcendent function for the client until the mother-child unity is symbolically restored.

Sandplay seems to assume a client can play. Yet when a client cannot yet play because the symbolic attitude is arrested, it is the task of the therapist to gradually bring the client into an experience of transitional space (Winnicott, 1971) where symbols can be put to use in play. The sandplay therapist must be able to understand the symbolic nature of countertransference experiences (which may come to her in the form of countertransference images, somatic delusions, affect or dissociative experiences) and hold the symbolic attitude regarding her countertransference. It is the slow, patient countertransferential *living through* with increasing understanding — metabolizing primitive wordless experience and making it symbolizable — that helps usher the dyad into transitional space.

So while it may not be experienced as such, the field of Original Oneness/Merger is actually a place of creative, fertile incubation. It is a place where, according to Winnicott (1945), the therapist "gathers up the 'bits and pieces' of the client's self so that the client will "feel integrated at least in the person of the analyst" (p. 150). It is a place of waiting for the good enough mothering experience to be internalized, for enough faith to allow some space and the eventual use of the symbol. It is difficult for the therapist, yes, and at times, almost unbearable. But this is a place where the therapist can make space to feel, sense, think about, and hold the client's "unthought known" (Bollas, 1987). This type of containment takes place in the therapist's *mindwomb* — her mental, visceral, emotional space for holding the client's affect and experience (Wrye, 2001) — through the use of reverie, holding, and mirroring. Healing occurs not only through sandplay but through our active though sometimes silent containing and understanding. Some clients will remain "stuck" for long periods of time, even years. Clinical experience with these clients shows that it's a matter of critical mass: when enough ego or resiliency is built up, they become unstuck. This normalizes the stuckness that sometimes occurs in all therapies, even in sandplay. Stuckness is an opportunity for metabolization of pre-symbolized affect. It is as if the client is silently asking, "Can you understand that what I am communicating is as yet unsymbolized?" and "Can you, within yourself, help me begin to symbolize it?" At these times the countertransference experience of meaninglessness may be the only source of the symbol.

Both Kalff (1980) and Winnicott (1960/1965a, 1963/1965b, 1963/1965c) emphasize a frame of real safety and security. If there is a secure frame, then it is *possible* to have play. The structure of sandplay, based on Kalff's *free and protected space,* invites play. Yet, from Winnicott we know that play is an internal capacity. For some patients there exists an internal bastion of stuckness and/or emptiness that cannot yet be "played" out in the symbolic realm of the sandtray. However, an in-between transitional space (paradoxically neither internal nor external) may be developed through the therapist's full experiencing and active containing of pre-symbolic processes in this field.

The field of Original Oneness/Merger, like the field of Twoness/Rupture discussed next, is a field of projective identification. These are fields in which unspeakable emotional experience is communicated nonverbally because, lacking an internalized sense of safety, the client cannot yet symbolize and play. The therapist cannot create complete safety by sheer will or even empathic skill, as these fields are *by definition* felt to be unsafe. Relational safety, especially after trauma, is built slowly and incrementally.

This is not to say that every traumatized client will work only within the fields of Original Oneness/Merger or Twoness/Rupture. Clearly, this is not the case. The sandplay literature provides many examples of severe early trauma being healed in Field Three, the field of Differentiated Oneness and Transitional Space, the *secured-symbolizing* field. I emphasize countertransference experience in Fields One and Two because until now they lay unexplored in the sandplay literature.

Fields One and Two probably occur less frequently in sandplay than Field Three. But these "other" fields may arise, even within a single session. The therapist who understands the full range of the experience and the work to be done in each field is better equipped than the therapist who believes that sandplay takes place only within the limits of transitional space. Our work benefits when we know there is not anything wrong with the therapy or with the therapist if the more immediate, "easy" empathy of transitional space is not present.

In Field One, the field of Original Oneness/Merger, the seemingly out-of-contact field, suffering that has no words is all the while being communicated. The therapist who understands this increases her capacity for holding, whether through verbal therapy or, sometimes, sandplay. It may not be possible at first to find the symbolic meaning in the sandplay image; often, the meaning may be captured only in the countertransference experience — the "image made flesh" (Samuels, 1989, p. 165). The *total situation,* the ambiance, and the background music of the relationship must be apprehended to find symbolic meaning in the field of Original Oneness/Merger, enabling us to hear our patient's silent cry.

Field Two: The Field of Twoness/Rupture

Field Two, the field of Twoness/Rupture, is also a field that brings forth early relational trauma. Here, we find ourselves embroiled in a struggle with disturbing unconscious contents, intense affect, and mutually activated complexes in the between and surround. It is a field of discomfort, conflict, and difficulty often evoking in the therapist a visceral, extremely disturbing experience.

The field of Twoness/Rupture is akin to Goodheart's (1980) *complex-discharging* field and to Ogden's (1994) paranoid-schizoid mode of experience. It tends to be the most distressing field encountered by sandplay therapists partly because it is strikingly different from the particular qualities of resonance that current sandplay literature (which mostly describes Field Three types of experience) would lead us to expect.

The therapist may identify the presence of this field "mainly by anxiety, tension and pressure which he feels emerging within himself with or without obvious coercion from the patient" (Goodheart, 1980, p. 8). We may feel attacked, either energetically or verbally, in the between and surround. We may feel taken over by a feeling of fear, terror, anxiety, rage, dread, self-doubt, physical illness, or shame about our abilities. "Rupture" refers to the ambient anxiety that empathic rupture is imminent. We fear that no matter how hard we try, we somehow fail to provide holding that avoids this rupture. Here, as in the field of Original Oneness/Merger, we often need to rely on our subjective experience to come to symbolic understanding.

Following is an example of a sandplay therapist's work with a client in the field of Twoness/Rupture:

Uncontainable Feelings Spew Forth: Grief and Rage

I have worked very deeply with one client, a young man, two or three times per week for many years. His mother died when he was quite young. His family's way of dealing with grief and other painful feelings was to repress the feelings and gruffly pretend that everything was all right. Any expression of emotion was cause for shame and humiliation. So, my client never grieved his mother's death.

In therapy, the first years were marked by a frozen negative transference, with my client withholding everything and refusing to trust me or the therapy process. During the next several years, the client began to feel his anger, his rage at his life, and his sadness. During this period, his feelings were almost uncontainable, the rage and grief pouring out like a volcano spewing hot lava. My ending his session — so akin to his family's injunction to shut down his feelings — was unbearably painful. It triggered a rage reaction so strong that he would slam the door and walk down the hall scraping his knuckles against the rough plaster until they bled. His rage toward me was quite intense; I was experienced as the abandoning mother, and the father forbidding him to have his feelings.

It was during this volatile period that he began making sand trays, spontaneously jumping off the couch to pace the room, and on several occasions, to approach the tray. Each time he began sandplay, the tension in the air was so thick it was crackling. His rage was so fierce and unpredictable that I felt deeply anxious and fearful. My body was so tense I could hardly breathe, and my stomach was in knots. However, when he approached the tray, something happened. He would stand in front of the tray for a while, quiet and pensive. Then he would reach for a pointed tool which he used like a pen. With this he would draw designs in the sand. Each time he created a tray, something inside of him would calm down. Working with the sand — in my mind, the sand as Mother Earth — calmed and soothed him. As he worked, I could feel my own tension relaxing, draining out, calming down. I could breathe again. When he finished the tray, he would quietly lay the instrument down and return to the couch. During his time at the tray, something in his body and in mine had been transformed. Afterward, he would be quiet and docile, able to talk openly for the remainder of the hour. Although the ends of these sessions were also painful and difficult, they lacked the sadistic self-hatred and hot rage of the other session endings.

Although I did not quite experience terror with this client, I was at times frightened and anxious for my physical safety. When he started going to the sand, I felt relief that he had found a way to soothe himself. (Cunningham, 2003, pp. 199-200)

This therapist is able to get to a symbolic understanding of her resonance and thereby able to better contain and mediate the intense and disturbing rage that enveloped the field, allowing for a temporary movement from Field Two into Field Three.

Unlike in Field One, relational trauma in Field Two is *relived* within the relationship rather than desperately avoided. In the field of Twoness/ Rupture, the client so intensely anticipates retraumatization that every word or move on the part of the therapist may be felt as traumatic. Vulnerable parts of the therapist are then triggered and the therapist may also feel traumatized in this field. Rather than "feeling with" the client, the therapist may experience a "feeling against" (Bradway & McCoard, 1997). The two individuals' complexes are activated and do a dance of discharge (Goodheart, 1980) and retraumatization.

Self State Sandtrays

Sandtrays made within the fields of Original Oneness/Merger and Twoness/Rupture — like Kohut's (1977) idea of a self state dream — often express "the nonverbal tensions of traumatic states," such as dread or fear of disintegration of the self (p. 109). Thus, for the therapist, symbolic understanding of the tray has to do with nameless anxieties. Such trays may be better understood symbolically in their entirety, in the pervasive feeling tone of fragmentation or annihilation. These sandtrays and the countertransference of devastation and futility that often accompanies them communicate the state of the patient's true self, hidden behind the non-communication of the false self. When we understand these trays as a visual image of the client's somatic-psychic experience of trauma, we are less likely to be traumatized by them. *(See Figures 2, 3 and 3a.)*

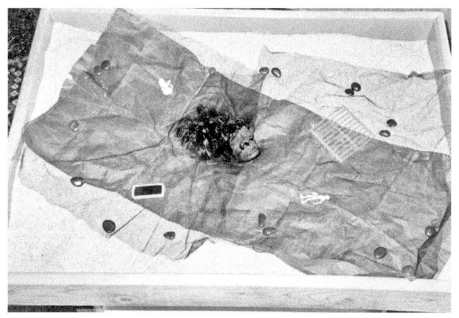

Figure 2: Self State Sandtray, conveying nameless dread. A black shrunken head sits in the middle of blue tissue paper, reminiscent of Kali and the river of death. Field Two of Twoness/Rupture.

Figures 3 and 3a: Self State Sandtray, conveying fear of disintegration of the self. Field Two of Twoness/Rupture, mingling with Field One dissociation.

The field of Twoness/Rupture was frequently apparent in the difficult cases provided by sandplay therapists, who were disturbed by their inability to provide a felt sense of the free and protected space. Often there was self-blame, a feeling of failure. The suffering experienced by sandplay therapists when encountering this field is strikingly different than what is purported in the sandplay literature. And yet, *where the therapist is most deeply affected is where great change occurs.* Thus, in this field, as with the Rainmaker, when we find a way to put ourselves right in the world of the transference/countertransference through gaining a meta-understanding of the situation, the field itself may gradually calm down, which of course effects change in the client as well.

Below is a description of work with one of my clients in the field of Twoness/Rupture in the verbal therapy and in the sandtray:

Nigredo Landscape

A delightful, lively yet often depressed young woman whose mother had been both "too much" and "too little" often spoke to me with a demanding, complaining tone. Yet she cherished her weekly sessions. It was clear that she came to me to *magically* fix her problems. She saw me as all-powerful, possessing a wisdom and magic she did not have. Without words, she urgently, desperately demanded that I help her.

Her sandplay process began with a coherent scene of a journey. It was full of light and clarity, an enchanting story in the sand. Then she rapidly descended into black despair and anger and remained in that emotionally dark and hopeless place for several years. I felt her unspoken demand for me to *do something,* to work some magic. But my feeling was that I was floundering. I felt agitated and stumped — a panicky, desperate, "I don't know what to do" feeling. Her sandtrays reflected chaos and darkness. I could see no movement. They were abstract, unbalanced and foreboding *(Figures 4, 5).* I was confused by them.

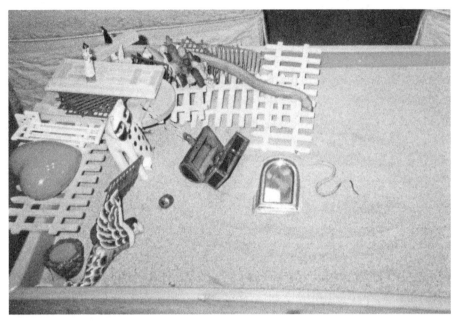

*Figure 4: Nigredo Landscape. Abstract, unbalanced, foreboding...
Field Two of Twoness/Rupture.*

*Figure 5: Nigredo Landscape. Chaos and darkness; countertransference
confusion. Field Two of Twoness/Rupture.*

In the field of Twoness/Rupture, all attempts at "feeling with" may fail. A disturbing countertransference, even a "feeling against," is common because the therapist is identified with an aspect of her client's internal world that she denies or rejects in herself (Racker, 1957/1972). When clients trigger deeply wounded aspects of ourselves that we do not want to face, we have a hard time "feeling with" unless we come to understand which aspect of our own internal world is being activated. Identifying this and internally working toward empathic understanding tends to resolve the experience of "feeling against," allowing the therapist to once again have empathy.

Even so, the therapist should not be too hasty in trying to regain footing in a symbolizing field. Some clients may need to frequently return or remain stuck in Field Two to resolve important relational issues. In these cases, the therapist is advised to "sustain the feelings which are stirred in him" (Heimann, 1950, p. 82). If "feeling with" is valued over "feeling against" the therapist may make leaps that diminish and foreclose the effectiveness of experiential awareness as a therapeutic tool.

During consultation on the case of *Nigredo Landscape,* I realized that I was defending against my own frantic, childlike, helpless feeling. I gradually became aware of this, as four different consultants gave me four very different kinds of advice. One — the "consultant" being an entire group — was dumbfounded. Another consultant advised me to recommend medication. Yet another advised me not to keep the client in therapy for too long because she was so young. I now believe there was a parallel process involved where two of my consultants felt my own desperate need to *do something!* Against this backdrop of advice to either medicate her or move her along quickly, my fourth consultant said, in effect, "Do nothing. Sometimes all we can do is to be with another in her pain." As this consultant calmed me, it became clearer to me that my own desperate need to help, designed to fend off my own vulnerability, resonated with my client's deep feelings of terror and helplessness. I then began to understand the nuances of meaning in her dark place. This negative transference/countertransference, and my frantic internal attempt at "climbing out" of the field rather than truly taking it in was a repetition of the original trauma: "... that of being in the care of a mother who, while filled with her own unbearable and undigested suffering, was unable to bear feeling her baby's suffering in relationship to her own human failings" (Mitrani, p. 1093). A poem my client had written at a much younger age helped me to understand her/our desperation:

> *Modaughter*
>
> *Strangled by a 21 year old*
> *umbilical cord.*
> *her*
> *blood feeds my veins*
> *her angst-ridden fears.*
> *I try to climb from*
> *her*
> *thick and stifling*
> *womb,*
> *but I must go down*
> *the birthing canal.*
> *contraction by contraction,*
> *push after push.*
> *silently, I scream.*
> *labor is endless.*
> *in exhaustion I dream of light and air.*

At a visceral level, I began to understand her suffocating, unmediated, unbearable experience of life, right from her very beginning as a preemie, and my own reluctance about going down the birth canal with her. Yet, down was the only way to go. My energetic attempts at pulling her up and trying to "help" were not helping at all. They were holding her longer in desperation and darkness. Gradually, I experienced consciously and symbolically the desperate urgency of her fight against being born.

To work therapeutically within the field of Twoness/Rupture, sandplay therapists need to understand it *symbolically*. In the act of projective identification, the client has put split-off unbearable experience into the therapist's body, placing it on the "hook" of the therapist's vulnerability or complex. The sandplay therapist needs to become conscious of her body's visceral experience and preconscious feeling states *as windows into the client's experience.* These countertransference experiences may gradually have symbolic meaning for the therapist, as they are understood *"from the inside out"* (Sands, 1997a, p. 664), and from the standpoint of Racker's (1957/1972) concept of complementary countertransference.

Next, we move to Field Three: The Field of Differentiated Oneness and Transitional Space. Paradoxically, all therapeutic space is potentially transitional space, but in the first two fields it may not *feel* transitional. Change in the first two fields is more tedious and slow, and yet change *does* occur. In these fields, it is the task of the therapist, while holding her countertransference experience as a bridge to the patient's internal world, to gradually symbolize her experience of the field, that is, to silently put words or image to what is at first only felt in the body.

However, I do not wish to limit countertransference to that which is unsymbolized, but to emphasize its importance in work with unsymbolized experience. We resonate with both symbolized and unsymbolized experience, and both are therapeutically useful.

Field Three: The Field of Differentiated Oneness/ Transitional Space

The field of Differentiated Oneness/Transitional Space holds the experience of fluent empathy where the unconscious minds of patient and therapist are aligned. It is the field of a "good analytic session" where there are rich layers of symbolic meaning, full associations, or meaningful silence.

The field of Differentiated Oneness and Transitional Space was, up until recently, the only field described in sandplay theory. It is usually experienced as "free and protected space" and often referred to as "co-transference," which Bradway has linked to Winnicott's transitional space and Goodheart's *secured-symbolizing* field (Bradway & McCoard, 1997). It is the field of seamless empathic connection and "feeling with." It is also the field of the meaningful use of the symbol and true play. It is the place that all therapists treasure because we feel effective and enlivened when we work in this field.

The essence of this field is symbolization. This is *differentiated* oneness —real connection and also separateness. It is a space in between, the space necessary for the symbol to emerge. Because of the more fluid symbolic understanding, early trauma may be re-experienced in a field of Differentiated Oneness and Transitional Space but will not feel so confusing or disturbing to the therapist. There will be flow and empathy in the between and surround. Perhaps one reason most published sandplay cases take place in this field is that sandplay itself very often *activates* the field of transitional space, where even trauma will be felt, recognized, and relatively easily understood. Countertransference amplifies this process.

Goodheart (1980) describes the *secured-symbolizing space* as one of:

> ...free mutual exploration of fantasy and reality, i.e., a setting in which patient and therapist can work collaboratively, predominantly through the use of symbols. In such a setting, even though the patient leads the way and is 'the patient,' both partners are intensely involved. However, each retains his identity, and neither patient nor therapist labors under complex expectations or pressures from the other. Communication in the fullest sense is present and is not subverted to coercion or to deception. This is the field where circumambulation of dream and fantasy, active imagination, non-verbal work with art materials or sandplay and clear discussion of transference experiences will occur virtually spontaneously, the patient almost falling into these activities by himself. (p. 9)

Ogden's (1994) description of the depressive position shares many of these qualities, especially when he says that the depressive position "generates a quality of experience endowed with a richness of layered symbolic meanings" (pp. 35-36)[29] along with an interpreting "I." Here, forms of defense, such as repression and mature identification (rather than the projective identification used in the other two positions), allow the individual to sustain psychological strain over time. Negative countertransference experience in this field is still likely to be a "feeling with," such as easily understood sadness, anger, or

---

[29] It is important to note that reaching the depressive position does not necessarily mean health; it is, rather, a more mature experiencing of anxiety. Being stuck in the depressive position is problematic. Psychological health is found in the easy oscillation and flow of muted experiences in all three positions: autistic-contiguous, paranoid-schizoid and depressive modes of experience.

angst. Projective identification and complementary countertransference in this field are rare, or quite subtle, and easily integrated through the readily available symbolic understanding.

Nigredo Landscape, Continued

The continuation of the case of *Nigredo Landscape* illustrates a shift from Field Two, the Field of Twoness and Rupture, into Field Three, the Field of Differentiated Oneness and Transitional Space. As I worked hard in consultation to understand my own experience of desperate inadequacy, I began to understand my client's uninterpretable trays as symbolic of her inner fragmentation and nameless anxieties. Perhaps these arose from her having been born prematurely and spending weeks in an incubator or, later, from her experience of her mother's constant and worsening illnesses and pervasive fears. As my own anxiety calmed and my desperate need to help diminished, my increasing understanding seemed to mark the beginning of her return from darkness.

> During this dark period she repeatedly became suicidal and was often afraid. At these times we had short daily telephone conversations. She told me that contact with me gave her something to look forward to and helped her feel better. Together, we had found a way for her to feel that she was not alone in this darkness.

> Several of her sandtrays held a huge Godzilla. Once, she deliberately (but unconsciously) turned its head at an awkward angle so that it was glaring at me from the corner of the tray that was nearest to me *(Figure 6)*. Other times she used a little doll with spiky black hair and an angry face holding a sign toward me that said "Protest!" *(Figure 7)*. I noticed that I felt relief at this unconscious demonstration of her feelings as they emerged from their hiding place within an intensely idealizing transference. During one session, she went to the shelves looking for birds. "You don't have enough birds," she said. Two weeks later she approached the shelves again. This time she said, "You have way too many birds."

> Rather than feeling confused or desperate, as I had earlier, I understood that — like her mother — I was being experienced as both too much and too little. I could feel that a monstrous anger was being expressed and transformed. As we weathered

this *nigredo* together, her experience of me gradually became that of an older, helpful woman who was simply human, rather than magically omnipotent or pitifully inadequate.

Figure 6: Godzilla. "Anger of monstrous proportions was being expressed and transformed." Field Two moving into Field Three of Differentiated Oneness /Transitional Space.

Figure 7: Protest! The "protest" felt familiar and tolerable. Moving into Field Three of Differentiated Oneness /Transitional Space.

Gradually, her trays became lighter in weight and color and *rubedo* entered the more integrated scenes. Frequently, the figure of Lucy in her counseling booth was there in the tray. On the booth it said, "The Doctor Is In" *(Figure 8a)*. And after many years, a peaceful centering appeared in the tray.

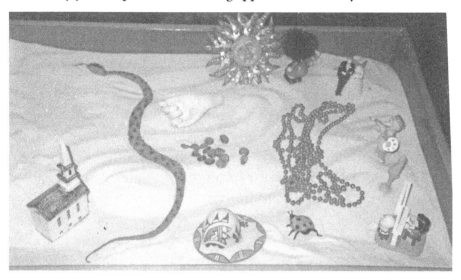

Figures 8 and 8a: The Doctor Is In. "The doctor" is becoming internalized as an experience of calm, consistency, reliability and trust. The nigredo is more integrated and rubedo enters the field. Field Three of Differentiated Oneness/Transitional Space.

More and more frequently we found ourselves in transitional space, The Field of Differentiated Oneness, the field of fluent empathy. By exploring (internally) my experience of this unique relational field, despite its discomforts, I was able to help her move into new ways of experiencing anxiety and making meaning.

Field Four: The Numinous Field

Field four, which I call the Numinous Field, arises from Field Three (O'Connell, 1986). Field Four is ever present in the holding of sacred space provided by the therapist. Yet Field Four also may manifest in a more obvious way as the transcendent function. It holds an awe-inspiring experience and a profound shift in attitude. When Field Four arises in this intensified way, both therapist and client are changed by it.

Figures 9 and 9a: Self Tray. Five turtles and a lotus blossom gather at the center.

Nigredo Landscape, continued

Continuing with the *Nigredo Landscape* case, notice the shift from Field Two to Field Three to Field Four. Out of the centering process that began two years earlier, a Self tray appears *(Figure 9)*. Five turtles and a lotus blossom hold the center of the tray, as symbols of loss and resilience meet in a fully symbolic, numinous field. When I saw this tray, I inwardly gasped, and then I silently rejoiced.

Another example of Field Four follows. This example illustrates a shift in fields from Oneness/Merger to Differentiated Oneness/Transitional Space, and finally into the Numinous Field.

> A young male client ruminated in the verbal therapy about his need to be an artist. He was persona-identified as a writer, and yet he was not writing. He desperately felt that writing would make him feel alive. He was quite drawn to sandplay, and interspersed with verbal sessions over a year and half, made eight sandtrays,

all quite stark and revealing his tremendous grief. This grief went back to his birth, and he wept as his losses and early relational trauma symbolically appeared in the sand. Whereas in the verbal therapy, I felt helpless and deadened, and was unable to help him find emotional meaning in his repetitive monologue, it was quite different when he worked in the sand. When he spoke after completing each sandtray, his voice became poetic, deep with feeling and understanding. The ambiance in the room shifted dramatically, and each time, I was deeply moved.

When he suddenly had a profound experience of the Self, we found ourselves immersed in goldenness in the room. I felt transported to another place, a timeless place. I had no words. We both felt it. More than anything else, I felt awe and gratitude for being allowed to participate in the mystery.

After this experience, his attitude toward life changed dramatically. His depression lifted, and his desperate need to identify as an artist fell away. He became more fully engaged as he began to *creatively live his life.*

The essence of the Field Four is numinous experience, often accompanied by a dramatic shift in attitude and the sense of awe that accompanies the constellation of the Self. Field Four is a shared, transcendent, relational experience of the union of conscious and unconscious, completely void of anxiety. At the same time, Field Four represents the ever-present container of numinous psychic holding provided by the therapist. The therapeutic goal, within this timeless container of shared psychic experience, is to gradually move into embodied, emotionally connected self-reflection, and to establish fluid oscillation between all four fields.

Summary of Part III

As a theoretical model that sheds light on some previously unexplored areas of clinical experience in sandplay, relational sandplay theory describes and gives meaning to a fuller range of countertransference experience for the sandplay therapist. It is intended to normalize difficult relational experiences, thereby helping sandplay therapists not only tolerate but more importantly *therapeutically use* material that might otherwise bring shame and self-doubt, or the misguided judgment of a "failed" sandplay process. It calms our anxieties to know that the sensory experiences of boredom, emptiness, and drowning in the field of Original Oneness/Merger and that the intensely affective, disturbing, or viscerally gripping experiences in the field of Twoness/Rupture *are normal.* It can be liberating to realize that our more disturbing countertransference experiences actually contain meaningful information that leads to healing.

These fields may be thought of as representing the deintegration and reintegration of the Self that happens continuously to most of us throughout life. After a Self experience, one cycles through other fields but with a stronger ego-Self axis and a more stable foundation from which to draw, making these experiences more muted and easily understood, more meaningful, and therefore less painful. Fordham (1957/1974) stressed the therapist's availability to deintegrate to more primitive states with the client — that is, to immerse oneself in the countertransference experience in whatever field it arises and to use it toward meaningful understanding.

It is my hope that this conceptualization of relational fields for sandplay therapy will help us work in these fields more skillfully. Work in any of these fields is legitimate and necessary therapeutic work. None of these fields is less creative, loving, or spiritual than any other. Each of these fields is held by the Self and is fertile in its own way, representing unique places of creative waiting in the mindwomb of the therapist.

Chapter 11

The Flow of Relational Energies in the Self: Qualities, Symbolic Meanings and Interventions

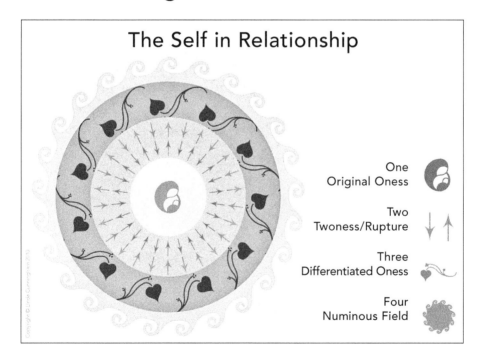

This diagram of the relational Self shows the Four Archetypal Relational Fields and their relationship to the Self, from Field One in the center, moving outwards through Field Two, Field Three and Field Four. These fields represent the somatic, emotional, symbolic, and spiritual realms of human relational experience, and the dynamic, constant flow of relational energies, as held by the Self. The fields depicted here represent both developmental stages and experiential states. Beginning in earliest childhood, development moves from the center to the periphery, as we develop the psychological capacities of each field, unless trauma prevents us from doing so. All of these relational fields are also normal aspects of human experience, and may be experienced fleetingly or for extended periods at any time in life. The therapeutic goal in all fields is to gradually move, through the therapist's use of self, into embodied, emotionally connected self-reflection, and to establish fluid oscillation between all four fields.

Field One: The Field of Original Oneness/Merger

In the diagram, the Field One area is in the center of the *Self In Relationship* circle. This area represents the somatic core of the Self. This field takes us into our bodies — or out of our bodies — but always involves sensory experience.

When trauma manifests in the clinical relationship, Field One qualities may be experienced for long periods of time. Following are the qualities of the field, possible symbolic meanings, and interventions.

Countertransference Qualities of Field One

Blankness, dizziness, confusion, deadness

Feeling of dissolving into space or a watery feeling

Feeling held at bay, ineffective

Boredom, sleepiness, anxiety, dissociation

Feelings of ineffectiveness

Symbolic Meanings of Field One

Early maternal deprivation

Need to establish basic trust, a secure base

Need for merger with a protective other

Fear of getting too close

Demand to be heard and seen

A silent cry

Projective identification of deadness or unnameable dread

Need to find one's edges

Frantic attempt to establish a well-integrated *persona*

Interventions in Field One

Silently incubate the countertransference

Use reverie

Interpret the field like you would a dream

Investigate your resonance: What is happening in my body? What might it mean?

The gaze: Facial expressions can convey empathy and safety when no words are permitted

Soft noises: "Ohhh" or "Ummmhmmmm"

Field Two: The Field of Twoness/Rupture

In the diagram, the Field Two area is the second ring from the center of the *Self In Relationship* circle. This area represents the *emotional* core of the Self. As with Field One, when trauma manifests in the clinical relationship, Field Two qualities may be experienced for long periods of time. Following are the qualities of the field, possible symbolic meanings, and interventions.

Countertransference Qualities of Field Two

Vitality; aliveness

Pressure to discharge the tension of interacting complexes

Disturbing unconscious contents

Discontinuity: Splitting and projective identification

Discomfort, difficulty, dread, anxiety, terror, rage, shame, or physical symptoms

Internal images of aggression, violence, abuse

Feelings of ineffectiveness

Symbolic Meanings of Field Two

Early maternal deprivation

Relational trauma

Normal developmental processes of separation have been derailed

Need to establish basic trust, a secure base

Fear of getting too close

Desperate feelings about unmet needs

The eruption of complexes

Interventions in Field Two

Empathy

Patience, holding, consistency, reliability, resilience

Repair empathic ruptures

Maintain calm in the face of the storm

Work with one's own resistance and complexes

Understand our own issues blocking therapeutic progress

Think symbolically about traumatic feelings and images

Set effective boundaries

Field Three: The Field of Differentiated Oneness/ Transitional Space

In the diagram, the Field Three area is represented by the third ring from the center in the *Self In Relationship* circle. This represents a more integrated somatic/emotional/symbolic-relational area of the Self. Field Three is rich in symbolic meaning, full associations, or meaningful silence. This field may be pervasive or intermittent. When it becomes more pervasive, the therapist knows that the capacity for trust and relational connection is flowering. Following are the qualities of the field, possible symbolic meanings, and interventions.

Countertransference Qualities of Field Three

Fluent, "easy" empathy

Feeling of connection

Meaningful resonance

Satisfaction with the therapeutic work

Feeling of going-on-being in the dyad

Symbolic Meanings of Field Three

Capacity for trust

Internalized image of the good mother

Growing secure attachment

Feelings and thoughts can be more consciously experienced

Ego-Self axis is intact

Transcendent functioning is possible, or likely occurring

Human relationship is safer, more comfortable, more secure

Capacity for curiosity is developing

"Unthought known" may still exist

Interventions in Field Three

Be *with* the flow of psychic energies

Open to the meaning of the symbols

Field Four: The Numinous Field

In the diagram, the Field Four area is the outer layer of the *Self In Relationship* circle. This area represents the ever-present, numinous container. Within this sacred holding, the union of conscious and unconscious arises as the transcendent function.

Countertransference Qualities of Field Four

Felt sense of the sacred container for the clinical work

Sense of awe

Transcendent experience

Complete lack of anxiety

Symbolic Meanings of Field Four

Therapist's appreciation of the sacred container

Transcendent function

Constellation or manifestation of the Self

Interventions in Field Four

Experience it fully

Be *with* the Other

Chapter 12

Case Examples:
An Exploration
of the Four Relational Fields

This mutually woven relational pattern is not visible or touchable as the sand picture is... It has an effect on the body and soul of the participants.

— Ruth Ammann, 1991

In this chapter, I describe two sandplay processes, noting the flow of relational fields. The first is a case that comes from my research.

Case One: Endless War and Destruction

There was a boy I worked with in therapy for a long time. His parents were going through a divorce, and he was angry about the many changes. He was particularly angry with his mother and his new stepsister. He was having frequent temper tantrums.

I sat with him week after week as he made sandtrays full of fighting, guns, and war. He used the sandtray to blow things up,

137

to make big explosions. Given his presenting problems, I did not know how much of it was his trying to identify with the masculine, his own anger toward his mother, or his expression of his father's anger toward the mother. But there was constant aggression in the tray. I was there having to be the container and the witness. Female figures in the tray were always in imminent danger of violence; they were being eaten by sharks, or getting shot at, or being blown up. It was difficult to hold and sometimes I wanted to make it nice or pretty it up or say something good about women. It is difficult to be with that kind of primitive wish to destroy everything. I kept thinking, "When is the feminine going to come in? When will it soften?" I often felt dread, a sick feeling, like "Aaagh, this again." It was always about violence and killing. I just knew how much anger and fury there was. And he didn't just make ten or twenty trays like this. He made about fifty.

Sometimes I felt a dread of him coming, knowing there would be more and more of this violence. I was really sick of it and bored with it. For months, he would destroy the tray after he'd made something. It was hard for me because I have so romanticized the sandtray, and he'd throw in a bunch of bricks before I'd photographed it!

But I just tried to be in the moment with him. Sometimes I felt angry that he'd destroyed the tray. But actually, we usually had a good time. We played a lot together. I would even make myself watch "The Simpsons" so that when he came in and asked me, "Hey, did you see Bart Simpson?" I could say, "Yeah, that was pretty good." So I vacillated between feeling confused and feeling hopeful. Sometimes I felt stimulated.

Then there was one tray where he seemed to come into his own identification with men. I thought it was a really good thing, and I felt really good about it. He seemed much more grounded with his dad after that tray. Soon after, he began to bury things and had me find them. One thing he buried over and over was a little mirror. Another was a dead tree, which I felt represented the death of his family as he had known it. It was a difficult case for me, because sometimes I felt like I didn't know what I was doing and I doubted my own abilities. His process hadn't followed the pattern of how I think sandplay should go: the integration of the opposites and coming to the centering of the Self. He continued to destroy his trays right up to the very end. His parents told me that he loved coming to therapy. Toward the end of his process, he made a sandtray with a wounded guy on a stretcher and this whole army on either side, protecting him. And I thought, "Wow, that is really a transformation for him. Now he can carry this wounded part of himself. And he has all these heroic males around him." And then he put another little creature on the stretcher with the wounded soldier. It was a little pink warrior person. I thought it was probably me.

This case gives us a feel of a therapist fluidly progressing through multiple fields with a child client. Field One boredom and Field Two dread ebb in and out of the therapist's experience. Then slowly, Field Three brings healing and a sense of meaning. The rapport between therapist and client is good, particularly in the verbal therapy, and clearly there was a deepening into transitional space with the use of sandplay. But it took a long time, and the therapist suffered during this time, doubting her own abilities. This countertransference doubt and suffering indicate that the therapeutic dyad is operating in one of the earlier fields. This stuck place in the therapy seems to be more of a field of Twoness/Rupture than Original Oneness/Merger, with the therapist's vulnerabilities being activated, in particular her self-doubt, dread, anger and inner struggle around the child's repetitive aggression and destruction of his sandplay. And yet, the therapist's boredom, confusion, and sense of inadequacy may indicate Field One experience as well. The move into Field Three and transitional space is gradual yet obvious.

Case Two: The Oriental Carpet
An Image of Relatedness and Longing[30]

Particular images, fantasies, and feelings color each therapy and give it a life of its own. These experiences in the between and surround, such as my internal image in the following case of the "oriental carpet," hold both personal and archetypal places of resonance and, if nurtured, may blossom into the fully symbolizing Fields Three and Four.

> In working with a woman who had suffered severe neglect as a child, her images of childhood were of a barren refrigerator, a half-empty orange juice glass sitting in a window sill covered with cockroaches, and a mattress that smelled of cat urine in the laundry room where she slept.
>
> Her earliest memory was of standing in her crib crying for her mother, arms outstretched, but no one ever came. She had only one memory of being physically touched as a child, and that was when her second grade teacher brushed her hair out of her eyes. She remembered the shame of going to school always disheveled and she had a lingering feeling that she somehow smelled bad. She told me these things matter of factly, with little feeling.
>
> It seemed to me that she wished to disappear, to become invisible. At times she dissociated, which I sensed because I sometimes "went with her," feeling foggy myself. She talked constantly, leaving little room for me to speak. When I did speak, she looked quite startled as if surprised that I was still there. Other than that, she rarely made eye contact. She elusively hid behind her wall of words or disappeared into thin air, protecting herself from closeness with me. This was the ambiance of our work in her therapy for two years. During this time, and continuing well into the fourth year, I frequently noticed that my entire body itched when I sat with her. The itch traveled from my scalp to my arms, legs, and face and I

---

[30] This case first appeared in *The Journal of Sandplay Therapy,* 1999, 8(1).

continuously scratched at it. I noticed that sometimes she was scratching herself, as well. I had no way to understand this at the time, except that I had this experience only with her, so I suspected it was meaningful.

In our third year, she often worked in the sand and we sat facing each other across the tray. She almost never used figures but molded the sand, wet or dry, moving it around, then reshaping it. As she touched the sand, the atmosphere in the room changed. She wept silently, and talked about her childhood. Memories and long buried feelings of grief and shame flowed into consciousness as she worked in the sand. In fact, this seemed to be the only way in which she could access these feelings. As feelings surfaced, she began to change. Slowly, the *solutio* process ushered us into the realm of feeling. She soon began making dramatic gains in her social and professional life — from basement clerk to Executive Director — and she began to make more eye contact with me. Yet she still lacked a romantic relationship with a man, and wondered if she would ever be "normal" enough to have one.

In the fourth year of her therapy, I noticed that my attention would sometimes abruptly come and go. I would be pulled away from the content of her communication to me and into a fantasy of a beautiful red oriental carpet on the floor between us. I could almost literally see it there. I enjoyed it. It brought color into the barren feeling of the room. But I also experienced it as intrusive. It wouldn't go away, and I felt guilty about not giving her my full attention.

Since it would not go away, I decided to attend to it, to be curious about it, to see what it could tell me about what was happening in me, in her, and between us. I noted my own associations to oriental carpets. The one in my living room at home gives me hours of pleasure. It is a beautiful red, with rivulets of aqua "water" running through it. It changes with the natural changes of light: vibrant in the morning, flat but engaging at noon, luminous, rich and mysterious by lamplight. I bought it when my husband was on a month-long backpacking trip: I was worried about him, I missed him, I wished for his return. The oriental carpet nurtured me in his absence. It was a little piece of the "between"—like a little garden, between home and wilderness, between me and him.

During the months that I was pondering the meaning of the red oriental carpet to myself, she wore two different bright red dresses. I had never seen her dressed in red before — nor since. Then she came to a session with red hair. I remember feeling delight that a glimmer of *rubedo* had entered the room. I wondered if she had sensed my longing for more color and richness. Had she felt it as a demand *from* me? Or was it a demand she put *into* me, because she wanted more color and richness for herself, treasures that were forbidden, and as yet unknown? I supposed it might be a manifestation of both our needs to be connected, to feel held and nurtured, and to feel important to the Other. The fabric of my imaginal oriental carpet was woven with the threads of our desires. So I turned my attention toward her disavowed longing — that deepest and most painful of feelings. As we explored it, she revealed her unbearable shame about her desire to be loved.

I had not told her about my internal image of an oriental carpet. But one day she casually told me that years ago her mother had promised her a new oriental carpet after the divorce. It was to be a new beginning. They would have the material and emotional riches that they had never had. But the oriental carpet never came. As I listened, I sat in amazement. Internally, my eyes grew wide. I was struck by how my countertransference vision of the oriental carpet held us in a richly symbolic and mutually meaningful ambiance, connecting her unconscious, my unconscious and the Unconscious.

Shortly thereafter, she began to demand more of the therapy. She began to look directly at me and talk *with* me instead of *at* me. I felt as if I had finally been invited into the room. We then delved into the richness of our relationship: her longing for me to care about her and the shame she felt about having any needs at all. The therapy deepened as we became involved in her feelings, her desires, her angers toward me. My attention now stayed riveted with her. Rarely did I have the oriental carpet fantasy, yet I remembered it fondly.

As she prepared to leave therapy in our sixth year together, she was feeling competent and assertive at work, she had started a relationship with a man, and she was much more related to me. She told me that she was surprised to realize something new. "I'm in love," she said. She blushed as she continued, "With myself." At another time she said, "I'm blossoming!"

How can I explain my own dissociation, my itching, her barren sandtrays, and the oriental carpet image that captures my attention? Relational fields hold the shared experience of image and feeling within each unique relationship. In this case, I will trace our emergence from the field of Original Oneness/Merger — a necessary containing and reparative experience for this client — into the field of Differentiated Oneness/Transitional Space.

The field of Original Oneness/Merger holds sensory experience, and often takes on a dissociated quality. It also holds experiences of shapes and edges that give one a sense of bodily containment by one's own skin. If as a child, one is not adequately held and one's affect and experiences not meaningfully contained, there may be a primitive fear of one's body leaking away into nothingness, falling forever, dissolving, evaporating into thin air, or spilling out uncontrollably (Mitrani, 2001, referring to the work of Winnicott, Bick and Tustin). These fears are thought to be connected to a traumatic awareness of bodily separateness from the mother before a symbolic container has sufficiently formed to tolerate and transform them. A "second skin" formation may make the client feel safe from dissolving or fragmenting. The itching she and I experienced in this field brought us into contact with the edges of her psyche-soma, bringing our attention to the skin surface of our bodies, as if a second skin had formed to contain us, to give an outline to our invisible, dissociated, disembodied selves. As we incessantly scratched ourselves, I was aware of how rarely she had been touched, and I spoke about that. My reverie of this experience contained her. I think of the itching as new energy and sensation coming to long neglected bodily surfaces, symbolic containment being viscerally experienced on the body's edges. Yet, it took time to build up and firmly establish a consistent and enduring experience of herself as held in the (m)Other — safely ensconced in the symbolic container of my mindwomb.

Relational fields imperceptibly flow into each other. My experience of the oriental carpet, as well as of the itching, began in the field of Original Oneness/Merger. Dissociation is one of the hallmarks of Field One, as are barren sandtrays. The therapist's struggle to make sense of this experience in the between and surround is common. As feelings began to flow — as if they were dug up from the sand — the release of long buried emotions heralded our entry into a very mild Field Two. From it, we eventually emerged in transitional space. The image of the oriental carpet appeared following a release of affect allowed by the incremental formation of a safe bodily-experienced container. My reverie helped create this container. Yet perhaps the experience of the soft shapes and edges of the sand itself also helped increase her bodily experience of containment and safety.

The appearance of the rich image of the oriental carpet in the barren field of Original Oneness/Merger also holds a numinous quality, indicating the ever-present containing power of Field Four. The release of feelings in Field Two gently carried us into Field Three, the field of Differentiated Oneness/Transitional Space. The oriental carpet is an image of transitional space or a garden of the soul (Ammann, 1994), symbolic of interwoven relational threads that repaired patterns of unmet longings. At first the image seemed to come from me, but then later it seemed to have come from her. I could think of it as a state of *participation mystique* in which we were both fused with a numinous image from the collective unconscious. I could also think of it as projective identification, a putting of her own richness and passion and longing,

144

and even her red hot anger into me — for safekeeping, for modification, and/or because it was undeveloped and intolerable for her. It is likely that my internal work with these projective identifications, gradually contained and given back in modified form, actually helped to pull us out of the trance-like experience of Oneness/Merger by returning to her bits of awareness, bits of herself.

Ultimately, the oriental carpet image came to represent her blossoming in a garden of healing. This particular image is, of course, just one of an infinite number of ways of experiencing the between and surround. Each relational field is a garden of the soul that we cultivate and nurture into the blossoming of Eros, relationship, and beauty. The garden is a place of activity where we dig in the soil, plant seeds, nurture and protect seedlings, provide adequate water and nourishment, and then prune dead branches and begin the cycle again. Yet the garden is also the container for this process, an alchemical vessel where transformation can occur (Ammann, 1994).

The colorful blossoming that occurred in the daily life of this client never appeared in her sandtrays. But this does not diminish the importance of the sandplay work in her therapy. Experiences and images of increasing aliveness appeared, instead, in potential space, the area of illusion created when two individuals engage deeply on sensory, emotional and numinous planes. We both brought all of ourselves to the relationship, conscious and unconscious parts alike, longing for wholeness. There, this richness of her soul resonated with mine in such a way that I could not forget, in my holding of her deprivation, that there was color and passion and life in her that could not yet consciously be seen or felt. Often I felt that I was in the presence of a promise — a promise from the place where our psyches met, merged in the longing for wholeness, in an image that had significance for love and relationship for both of us. It was a promise of the Self, an image of Wholeness that also held the despair and disappointment of the broken promise of the past, and of her undeveloped potential.

The oriental carpet that "never came" was constellated between us. This image of relationship holds warp and weft, conscious and unconscious, home and wilderness, and, between us, wove something that could better withstand the sometimes careless footsteps of human beings. It brought her earned secure attachment.

As we work inside our own subjective experience of relational fields, we may resonate with Jung's words:

> The unrelated human being lacks wholeness, for he can achieve wholeness only through the soul, and the soul cannot exist without its other side, which is always found in a 'You.' Wholeness is a combination of I and You, and these show themselves to be parts of a transcendent unity whose nature can only be grasped symbolically.... (Jung, 1946, p. 82-83)

Chapter 13

Implications for Clinical Work

"Negative capability" is the ability to be in uncertainty, mysteries and doubts, without any irritable reaching after fact and reason... remaining content with half knowledge.

— *Keats*

Those who have experienced early relational trauma do not approach the unconscious with curiosity. Instead, anxiety and dissociation may reign. Thus, these clients may be reluctant to touch the sand, to deepen into a therapeutic process. They depend on the therapist to offer patience, symbolic understanding of their stuckness and trauma, the ability to suffer with them in pre-symbolic relational fields, and a benevolent holding of even the most disturbing subjective experience.

The therapist's subjective experience in sandplay is usually delightful, awe inspiring, and deeply satisfying. But when we are faced with unbearable countertransference experience, the Self is calling us to embrace this experience, too — to contain it, to make meaning of it in the service of Wholeness. Within the numinous field and a loving, symbol-making psychic embrace, we use the full range of our sensory, somatic, emotional, and thinking experience. We *practice* sitting in uncertainty and not knowing. Using mindfulness, we stay in the present moment of both conscious and unconscious communication between self and other, and we calm ourselves, using deliberate nonjudgmental attention to experience in the present moment.

Maintaining the Kalffian Sensibility

The field theory presented in this book adds a layer of complexity to Kalffian theory. However, the fundamental assumptions in sandplay are still relevant. They are as follows:[31]

The Clinical Attitude

The clinical attitude in sandplay is one of faith that the psyche, given the right conditions, is self-healing. The emphasis on the nonverbal, symbolic work in the sand is grounded in the understanding that it is the experience itself which heals, not the conscious understanding of it.

The therapist always provides the free and protected space — a loving maternal holding of the sacred space of therapy. He/she practices a receptive openness to the patient and to unconscious energies as they emerge, and allows this emergence in its own time and in its own way, without interfering with the creative process.

Of primary importance in this work is the sense of a living connection to the Sacred. The therapist focuses on the archetypal meaning of the symbols that arise within the personal context of the client. Through deep empathic connection with the client, the therapist performs the all-important task of *working toward symbolic understanding* of the patient and the patient's flow of images in the sand. This work is held within a positive transference, encouraged by the client's experience of freedom and protection that heals early injuries to the mother-child unity.

---

[31] This material first appeared in the *Journal of Sandplay Therapy* (2007), XVI(2).

Theoretical Understanding of Sandplay Process

In sandplay, unconscious processes are expressed in concrete, visible form. These energies appear in the form of "living symbols," touching upon the personal and collective unconscious, leading to spontaneous healing in the unconscious (Lauren Cunningham, 2004). The process tends to descend more and more deeply into the unconscious. In this descent, the freeing up of blocked psychic energies may be visible in the tray as contact with archetypal energies transforms the relationship between consciousness and the unconscious. In the deepest moment of the work, the constellation or manifestation of the Self may occur. This is considered to be the most important moment in healing as the ego takes its place in relation to the Self. There is then a return to a more integrated state. In this way, the Jungian individuation process leading to Wholeness in the personality is visible in sandplay.

Play, the great mediator between conscious and unconscious, facilitates a regression to the mother-infant unity and healing on the matriarchal level of consciousness.

Technique in Sandplay

In this method, the sandtray is the container of the individual soul. Work with groups, families, or couples in sandplay may be quite healing, but these are not within the auspices of Kalffian sandplay. Likewise, no techniques are used for making the unconscious conscious (such as active imagination or Gestalt techniques between figures in the tray, or verbal interpretation by the therapist). Verbal interpretation of the contents of the tray is postponed until after the sandplay process is finished, sometimes for years, because verbal interpretation violates the creative space and interrupts un-selfconscious play. Verbal interpretation pulls the client back into left brain thinking and can abort the right brain process so crucial to deep healing that sandplay provides. The therapist may interpret to herself, internally, but not verbally. Any verbal interpretation is about the external life situation of the client.

Training for the Therapist

The sandplay therapist must embrace and deepen his/her own psychological and spiritual growth. In the beginning, it is paramount that the therapist do his/her own sandplay process, and then continue to deepen his/her knowledge of the archetypal meaning of symbols through ongoing research and personal experience. It is also necessary that the therapist engage in ongoing training and study.

Evolving Theory in Sandplay

Sandplay has extraordinary powers to catalyze healing. Sandplay theory is actively deepening its exploration of the archetypal need for relatedness, and at the same time expanding its branches to connect with other theories. As the theory evolves, there is an emerging, more explicit recognition of issues of transference/countertransference and the nuances of the therapeutic relationship. Cases that include more explicit use of countertransference to understand preverbal/nonverbal material are showing up in the literature.

In that vein, the most important clinical implication of this book is its focus on the archetypal imperative of human relatedness. Clinically, our work with our own self in relation to our clients fosters and nurtures relatedness. Research shows that many therapists do *suffer with* their clients, even with the use of sandplay, and there is increasing evidence from neuroscience and attachment theory that Jung was correct in stating that this is the essence of healing.

In these times, many of our clients suffer from deep anxieties. Use of countertransference as a clinical tool was developed so that psychotherapy could reach a broader range of people, including those who suffer from unsymbolized experience: including thoughts that cannot be thought and feelings that cannot be felt — so common for those who have suffered early relational trauma.

Even so, in the world of countertransference the therapist is always a beginner. The meaning of countertransference is not truly, definitively knowable. It is ephemeral — a momentary flicker from implicit realms.

We can only seek to put fluid symbolic meaning onto the somatic or emotional points of light.

Because the sand itself is not relational, sandplay theory has needed to place more emphasis on the therapeutic relationship. It has needed a more detailed elucidation of recognizing, living through, and using the therapist's subjective experience in the between and surround, which has been so helpful in the contemporary psychoanalytic and Jungian approaches to verbal therapy. As we work more relationally, we may come to understand Jung's words more deeply:

Every genuine encounter between two human beings
must be conceived as a Mysterium Coniunctionis.
The living mystery of life is always hidden between Two.

— *C. G. Jung, 1979, p. 125*

References

Amatruda, K., & Helm Simpson, P. (1997). *Sandplay, the sacred healing: A guide to symbolic process.* Taos, New Mexico: Trance Sand Dance Press.

Amatruda, K. (1997). The world where worlds meet. *Journal of Sandplay Therapy, VI*(2), 19-24.

Ammann, R. (1994). The sandtray as garden of the soul. *Journal of Sandplay Therapy, IV*(1), 47-65.

Ammann, R. (1991). *Healing and transformation in sandplay: Creative processes made visible.* La Salle, IL: Open Court.

Aron, L. (1996). *A meeting of minds: Mutuality in psychoanalysis.* New Jersey: The Analytic Press.

Astor, J. (1995). *Michael Fordham: Innovations in analytical psychology.* London: Routledge.

Bacall, H. (1997). The analyst's subjectivity—How it can illuminate the analysand's experience: Commentary on Susan H. Sands' paper. *Psychoanalytic Dialogues, 7*(5), 669-681.

Berman, B. (1993). Symbols in the sand: An exploration of the initial sandworlds of female incest survivors. (Doctoral dissertation, California Institute of Integral Studies, 1993). *Dissertation Abstracts International, 54/09, 4907. Accession number: 9405109.*

Bick, E. (1968). The experience of the skin in early object relations. *International Journal of Psycho-Analysis, 49,* 484-486.

Bion, W.R. (1959a). Group dynamics: A review. *In Experiences in groups* (pp. 141-192). New York: Basic Books. (Original work published 1952)

Bion, W.R. (1959b). Attacks on linking. *International Journal of Psycho-Analysis, 40,* 308-315.

Bion, W.R. (1962a). *Learning from experience.* New York: Basic Books.

Bion, W.R. (1962b). A theory of thinking. *International Journal of Psycho-Analysis, 43,* 306-310.

Bion, W.R. (1977). Elements of psycho-analysis. In *Seven servants* (Chap. 11-13, pp. 48-63). New York: Jason Aronson. (Original work published 1963)

Bion, W.R. (1988). Notes on memory and desire. In E. B. Spillius (Ed.), *Melanie Klein Today* (Vol. 2, pp. 17-21). New York: Routledge. (Original work published 1967)

Bollas, C. (1987). *The shadow of the object: Psychoanalysis of the unthought known.* London: Free Association Books.

Bradway, K. (1991). Transference and countertransference in sandplay therapy. *Journal of Sandplay Therapy, 1*(1), 25-43.

Bradway, K., & McCoard, B. (1997). *Sandplay: Silent workshop of the psyche.* London: Routledge.

Cameron, S. (2003). Recognizing the appearance of the Self in sandplay therapy. *Journal of Sandplay Therapy, XII(1),* 133-141.

Campbell, N. (2004). *The Psychotherapy Institute Newsletter.* Berkeley, California.

Chiaia, M.E. (1998). Losing and finding: One child's experience of mourning. *Journal of Sandplay Therapy, VII(2),* 93-111.

Chiaia, M.E. (2001). Meeting and creative emergence: The silent interpenetrating mix of therapist and patient. *Journal of Sandplay Therapy, X(2),* 19-41.

Chodorow, J. (Ed.). (1997). *Encountering Jung: Jung on active imagination* (pp. 1-20). Princeton, NJ: Princeton University Press.

Cunningham, L. (1997). The therapist's use of self in sandplay: Participation mystique and projective identification. *Journal of Sandplay Therapy, 5*(2), 121-135. (German translation: Einsatz des Selbst durch den Sandspiel-Therapeuten: Participation Mystique and Projektive Identifikation. Zeitschrift Fur Sandspiel Therapie. Heft 9 Marz, 2000. (German publication of 1997 article.)

Cunningham, L. (1999). The oriental carpet: The interweaving of projective identification and participation mystique. *Journal of Sandplay Therapy, 8*(1), 69-74.

Cunningham, L. (2003). *Countertransference in sandplay: a symbolic / clinical approach.* (Doctoral Dissertation, California Institute of Integral Studies, UMI Dissertaton Services. UMI Number 3080414.

Cunningham, Lauren. (2004). *What is Sandplay Therapy?* STA Website: www.sta.org. http://www.sandplayusa.org/whatis.html. 1/28/04.

Dalenberg, C. (2000). *Countertransference and the treatment of trauma.* Washington, DC: American Psychological Association.

Deri, S. (1978). Transitional Phenomena: Vicissitudes of Symbolization and Creativity. In Grolnick, S. A. and Barking, L., Eds. *Between Reality and Fantasy: Transitional Objects and Phenomena,* pp. xx-xx. New York: Jason Aronson.

Donelan, J. (1999). What makes sandplay unique? Sandplay therapists' views on how sandplay relates to verbal techniques and the beneficial effects of using these modalities concurrently. *Dissertation Abstracts International, 60/09, 4884.* Accession number: 9945872.

Eigen, M. (1998). *The psychoanalytic mystic.* Free Association Books, Ltd., London.

Epstein, L., & Feiner, A. (1993). *Countertransference: The therapist's contribution to the therapeutic situation* (p. 1 - 23). Northvale, NJ: Jason Aronson.

Fonagy, P. (2001). *Attachment theory and psychoanalysis.* New York: Other Press.

Fordham, M. (1974). *Notes on the transference: Technique in Jungian analysis* (Vol. 2, pp. 111-151). London: William Heinemann Medical Books. (Original work published 1957)

Fordham, M. (1988). The infant's reach. *Psychological Perspectives, 21,* 58-76.

Fordham, M. (1993). Analytical psychology and countertransference. In L. Epstein & A. Feiner (Eds.), *Countertransference: The therapist's contribution to the therapeutic situation* (pp.193-209). Northvale, NJ: Jason Aronson.

Freud, S. (1953). The interpretation of dreams. In J. Strachey (Ed. & Trans.), *The standard edition of the complete psychological works of Sigmund Freud* (Vols. 4-5). London: Hogarth Press. (Original work published 1900)

Freud, S. (1957). The future prospects of psycho-analytic therapy. In J. Strachey (Ed. & Trans.), *The standard edition of the complete psychological works of Sigmund Freud* (Vol. 11, pp. 141-151). London: Hogarth Press. (Original work published 1910)

Freud, S. (1958). Recommendations to physicians practicing psychoanalysis. In J. Strachey (Ed. & Trans.), *The standard edition of the complete psychological works of Sigmund Freud* (Vol. 12, pp. 111-120). London: Hogarth Press. (Original work published 1912)

Freud, S. (1958). The disposition to obsessional neurosis. In J. Strachey (Ed. & Trans.), *The standard edition of the complete psychological works of Sigmund Freud* (Vol. 12, pp. 313-326). London: Hogarth Press. (Original work published 1913)

Goodheart, W. (1980). Theory of analytic interaction. *San Francisco Jung Institute Library Journal, 1*(4), 2-39.

Gordon, R. (1965). The concept of projective identification: An evaluation. *Journal of Analytical Psychology, 10*(2), 127-149.

Grosskurth, P. (1986). *Melanie Klein: Her world and her work.* Northvale, New Jersey: Jason Aronson, Inc.

Hall, J. (1984). Dreams and transference/countertransference: The transformative field. In N. Schwartz-Salant & M. Stein (Eds.), *Transference/countertransference* (pp. 31 -51). Wilmette, Il: Chiron.

Heimann, P. (1950). On countertransference. *International Journal of Psycho-Analysis, 31,* 81-84.

Hunter, V. (1998). Symbolic enactments in countertransference. *Psychoanalytic Review. 85*(5), 747-760. Abstract.

Irvine, C. (1999, October). *Complexes: The splinter psyches.* Paper presented at Intersection between Jung and Psychoanalysis Seminar, C.G. Jung Institute, San Francisco, California.

Jackson, B. (1991). Before reaching for the symbols dictionary. *Journal of Sandplay Therapy, 1*(1), 55-60.

Joseph, B. (1985). Transference: The total situation. *International Journal of Psycho-Analysis, 66,* 447-454.

Jung, C. G. (1954). Fundamental questions of psychotherapy. In H. Read, M. Fordham, & G. Adler (Eds.), R. F. C. Hull (Trans.), *The Collected Works of C.G. Jung,* (Vol. 16, pp. 111-125). Princeton: Princeton University Press. (Original work published 1951)

Jung, C. G. (1961b). *Memories, dreams and reflections.* New York: Vintage Books.

Jung, C. G. (1963). Mysterium coniunctionis. In H. Read, M. Fordham & G. Adler (Eds.), R. F. C. Hull (Trans.), *The Collected Works of C. G. Jung, 14.* Princeton: Princeton University Press. (Original work published 1955-1956)

Jung, C. G. (1966). *The psychology of the transference.* R. F. C. Hull (Trans.), Princeton, NJ: Princeton University Press. (Original work published 1946)

Jung, C. G. (1973). *Letters.* Volume I. Princeton: Princeton University Press.

Jung, C. G. (1979). *Word and image.* A Jaffe (Ed.) Princeton: Princeton University Press.

Kabat-Zinn, J. (2005). *Coming to our senses : Healing ourselves and the world through mindfulness.* New York: Hyperion.

Kalff, D. (1980). *Sandplay: A psychotherapeutic approach to the psyche.* Boston: Sigo Press.

Kalff, D. (1991). Introduction to sandplay therapy. *Journal of Sandplay Therapy, I*(1), 9-15.

Kalff, M. (1993). Twenty points to be considered in the interpretation of a sandplay. *Journal of Sandplay Therapy. II*(2), 17-35.

Kalsched, D. (1996). *The inner world of trauma: Archetypal defenses of the personal spirit.* London: Routledge.

Keats, J. (1973). From a letter to George and Thomas Keats. In J. Paul Hunter (Ed.), *The Norton introduction to literature: Poetry* (pp. 477-478). New York: W. W. Norton. (Original letter December 21,1817)

Klein, M. (1946). Notes on some schizoid mechanisms. *International Journal of Psycho-Analysis, 27,* 99-110.

Klein, M. (1952). The origins of transference. *International Journal of Psycho-Analysis. 33,* 433-438.

Klein, M. (1968). A contribution to the psychogenesis of manic-depressive states. In *Contributions to psycho-analysis, 1921-1945* (pp. 282-311). London: Hogarth Press. (Original work published 1935)

Kohut, H. (1959). Introspection, empathy and psychoanalysis. *Journal of the American Psychoanalytic Association, 7,* 459-483.

Kohut, H. (1971). *The analysis of the self.* New York: International Universities Press.

Kohut, H. (1977). *The restoration of the self.* New York: International Universities Press.

Langs, R. (1978a). *The listening process.* New York: Jason Aronson.

Langs, R. (1978b). *Technique in transition.* New York: Jason Aronson.

Langs, R. (1979). *The therapeutic environment.* New York: Jason Aronson.

Langs, R. & Searles, H. (1980). *Intrapsychic and interpersonal dimensions of treatment: A clinical dialogue.* New York: Jason Aronson.

Little, M. (1957). "R"— The analyst's total response to his patient's needs. *International Journal of Psycho-Analysis, 38,* 240-254.

Lukas, B. (2001). *What is Jungian child psychotherapy? Integrating sandplay and transference-countertransference.* Unpublished paper.

Machtiger, H. G. (1982). Countertransference/transference. In M. Stein (Ed.), *Jungian analysis* (pp. 86-110). Chicago, IL: Open Court.

Margoliash, E. (1998). Rebirth through sand. *Journal of Sandplay Therapy, VII*(1), 63-87.

McDougall, J. (1993). Primitive communication and the use of countertransference. In L. Epstein & A. Feiner (Eds.), *Countertransference: The therapist's contribution to the therapeutic situation.* (pp. 267-303). Northvale, NJ: Jason Aronson.

Miller, R. (1979). *Investigation of a psychotherapeutic tool for adults: the sandtray.* Unpublished doctoral dissertation, California School of Professional Psychology, Fresno, CA.

Mitchell, R.R., & Friedman, H. S. (1994). *Sandplay: Past, present and future.* London: Routledge.

Mitchell, S. (1997). *Influence and autonomy in psychoanalysis.* Hillsdale, NJ: The Analytic Press.

Mitchell, S. (2000). *Relationality: From attachment to intersubjectivity.* Hillsdale, NJ: The Analytic Press.

Mitrani, J. (2001). 'Taking the transference': Some technical implications in three papers by Bion. *International Journal of Psycho-Analysis, 82,* 1085-1104.

Montecchi, F. (1999). Hands that talk and analytic listening. *Journal of Sandplay Therapy, VIII*(1), 25-67.

Neumann, E. (1973). *The child.* New York: Jung Foundation for Analytical Psychology.

O'Connell, C. (1986). *Amplification in context: The interactional significance of amplification in the secured-symbolizing/context-plus field.* Unpublished doctoral dissertation, California Institute for Clinical Social Work, Berkeley, CA.

Ogden, T. (1982). *Projective identification and psychotherapeutic technique.* Northvale, NJ: Jason Aronson.

Ogden, T. (1986). *The matrix of the mind: Object relations and the psychoanalytic dialogue.* Northvale, NJ: Jason Aronson.

Ogden, T. (1989). *The primitive edge of experience.* Northvale, NJ: Jason Aronson.

Ogden, T. (1994). *Subjects of analysis.* Northvale, NJ: Jason Aronson.

Orange, D. (1995). *Emotional understanding: Studies in psychoanalytic epistemology.* New York: The Guilford Press.

Orange, D., Atwood, G., & Stolorow, R. (1997). *Working intersubjectively: Contextualism in psychoanalytic practice.* Hillsdale, NJ: The Analytic Press.

Pattis, E. (2002). What can a Jungian analyst learn from sandplay? *Journal of Sandplay Therapy, XI*(1). (Translated by Henry Martin) 29-41.

Racker, H.E. (1953). A contribution to the problem of countertransference. *International Journal of Psycho-Analysis, 34,* 313-324.

Racker, H.E. (1968). *Transference and countertransference.* New York: International Universities Press.

Racker, H.E. (1972). The meaning and uses of countertransference. *Psychoanalytic Quarterly, 26,* 303-357. (Original work published 1957)

Rocco, P. (2000). In place of words. *Journal of Sandplay Therapy, IX*(1), 45-64.

Samuels, A. (1985). *Jung and the post-Jungians.* London: Routledge.

Samuels, A. (1989). *The plural psyche: Personality, morality and the father.* London: Routledge.

Samuels, A. (1993). *The political psyche.* London: Routledge.

Samuels, A., Shorter, B., & Plaut, F. (1986). *A critical dictionary of Jungian analysis.* London: Routledge.

Sands, S. (1997a). Self psychology and projective identification—Wither shall they meet? A reply to the editors. *Psychoanalytic Dialogues, 7*(5), 651- 668.

Sands, S. (1997b). Protein or foreign body? Reply to commentaries. *Psychoanalytic Dialogues, 7*(5), 691-706.

Scharff, J. (1992). *Projective and introjective identification and the use of the therapist's self.* New Jersey: Jason Aronson.

Schore, A. (2003). *Affect regulation and the repair of the self.* New York: W. W. Norton & Company.

Schwartz-Salant, N. (1988). Archetypal foundations of projective identification. *Journal of Analytical Psychology, 33,* 39-59.

Schwartz-Salant, N. (1995). On the interactive field as analytic object. In M. Stein (Ed.), *The interactive field in analysis,* Wilmette, IL: Chiron, I, 1-36.

Searles, H. (1965). *Collected papers on schizophrenia and related subjects.* New York: International Universities Press.

Searles, H. (1979a). Feelings of guilt in the psychoanalyst. In *Countertransference and related subjects* (pp. 28-35). New York: International Universities Press. (Original work published 1966)

Searles, H. (1979b). Some aspects of unconscious fantasy. In *Countertransference and related subjects* (pp. 267-281). New York: International Universities Press. (Original work published 1973)

Searles, H. (1979c). *Countertransference and related subjects: Selected papers.* New York: International Universities Press.

Sedgwick, D. (1994). *The wounded healer: Countertransference from a Jungian perspective.* New York: Routledge.

Siegel, D. (1999). *The developing mind: how relationships and the brain interact to shape who we are.* New York, NY: The Guilford Press.

Siegel, D. (2004). The Process of Change in Psychotherapy: the links between neurobiology, subjective experience, and human relationships. Conference sponsored by Marin CAMFT, April 24, 2004, San Rafael, California.

Signell, K. (1990a). The use of sandplay with men. In G. Hill (Ed.), *Sandplay studies: Origins, theory and practice* (pp.101-132). Boston: Sigo Press. (Originally published 1981)

Signell, K. (1990b). The sandplay process in one man's development. In G. Hill (Ed.), *Sandplay studies: Origins, theory and practice* (pp. 157 - 194). Boston: Sigo Press. (Originally published 1981)

Slochower, J. (1991). Variations in the analytic holding environment. *International Journal of Psycho-Analysis, 72,* 709-718.

Slochower, J. (1996). Holding and the fate of the analyst's subjectivity. *Psychoanalytic Dialogues, 6* (3), 323-353.

Speigelman, M. & Mansfield, V. (1996). On the physics and psychology of the transference as an interactive field. In *Psychotherapy as mutual process* (pp. 183-207). Arizona: New Falcon Press.

Stevens, B. (1986). A Jungian perspective on transference and countertransference. *Contemporary Psychoanalysis 22,* 2.

Stewart, L.H. (1987). *Affect and archetype in analysis. In Archetypal processes in psychotherapy.* Wilmette, IL: Chiron.

Stolorow, R. (1988). Intersubjectivity, psychoanalytic knowing and reality. *Contemporary Psychoanalysis, 24,* 331-338.

Stolorow, R., Orange, D., & Atwood, G. (1997) Projective identification begone! *Psychoanalytic Dialogues, 7*(5), 719-725.

Stone, H. (1980). Prologue. In Kalff, D. (1980). *Sandplay: A psychotherapeutic approach to the psyche.* Boston: Sigo Press (pp. 9-22).

Sullivan, B. S. (2010). *The mystery of analytic work : Weavings from Jung and Bion.* New York: Routledge.

Symmington, N. & Symmington, J. (1996). *The clinical thinking of Wilfred Bion.* London: Routledge.

Tansey, M., & Burke, W. (1989). *Understanding countertransference: From projective identification to empathy.* Hillsdale, NJ: The Analytic Press.

Von Franz, M. L. (1980). *Projection and recollection in Jungian psychology.* La Salle: Open Court Publishing Co.

Wallin, D. J. (1999). Intersubjectivity and relational theory: How the new paradigm transforms the way we work. Unpublished course handout. Berkeley, California, April 25, 1999.

Wallin, D. J. (2007). *Attachment in Psychotherapy.* New York: The Guilford Press.

Weinrib, E. (1983). *Images of the self.* Boston, MA: Sigo.

Winnicott, D.A. (1958). Primitive emotional development. In *Through paediatrics to psycho-analysis* (pp.145-156).New York: Basic Books. (Original work published 1945)

Winnicott, D.A. (1965a). Ego distortions in terms of true and false self. In *Maturational processes and the facilitating environment,* (pp. 140-152). New York: International Universities Press. (Original work published 1960)

Winnicott, D.A. (1965b). Psychiatric disorder in terms of infantile maturational processes. In *Maturational processes and the facilitating environment,* (pp. 230-241). New York: International Universities Press. (Original work published 1963)

Winnicott, D.A. (1965c). Dependence in infant-care, in child-care, and in the psycho-analytic setting. In *Maturational processes and the facilitating environment,* (pp. 249-259). New York: International Universities Press. (Original work published 1963)

Winnicott, D.A. (1971). *Playing and reality.* New York: Basic Books.

Winnicott, D.A. (1982a). Hate in the countertransference. In *Through paediatrics to psycho-analysis* (pp. 194-203). London: Hogarth. (Original work published 1947)

Winnicott, D.A. (1982b). Primary Maternal Preoccupation. In *Through paediatrics to psycho-analysis* (pp. 300-305). London: Hogarth. (Original work published 1956)

Winnicott, D.A. (1982c). Transitional objects and transitional phenomena. In *Through paediatrics to psycho-analysis* (pp. 229-242). New York: Basic Books. (Original work published 1951)

Winter, R. (2000). The elusive "other" is found in the tray. *Journal of Sandplay Therapy, IX* (2), 27-52.

Wolstein, B. (Ed.). (1988). *Essential papers on countertransference* (pp. 1-15). New York: New York University Press.

Wrye, H. K. (2001). What's love got to do with it? Forms of Eros in the transference and countertransference. Presentation at The Psychotherapy Institute, Berkeley, California, October 27, 2001.

Index

About the Author

Linda Cunningham Ph.D., MFT, is a psychotherapist and consultant in San Francisco and Marin County, California.

She is passionate about her work with adults in depth psychotherapy. Many of her clients choose to do sandplay processes within their more verbal therapy.

Dr. Cunningham has taught contemporary psychoanalytic and Jungian theory as well as sandplay for many years, integrating them through the lens of countertransference. She is adjunct faculty at The California Institute for Integral Studies and in the Sonoma State University Depth Psychology Graduate Program. She teaches throughout the Bay Area in both graduate and postgraduate settings, and has presented her work with sandplay both nationally and internationally. She is a certified teaching member of the Sandplay Therapists of America and The International Society of Sandplay Therapists.

Dr. Cunningham offers trainings focused on different aspects of the clinical relationship, such as countertransference, the four relational fields, dreamwork, Jungian theory and practice, and sandplay. For information, see www.drlindacunningham.com or www.relationalsandplaytherapy.com.

Sandplay and the Clinical Relationship

CPSIA information can be obtained
at www.ICGtesting.com
Printed in the USA
BVHW010104290719
554523BV00021B/147/P